The Cost of Choice

The Cost of Choice
Women Evaluate
the Impact of Abortion

Preface by
Jean Bethke Elshtain

Edited by
Erika Bachiochi

ENCOUNTER BOOKS
SAN FRANCISCO

First edition published in 2004 by Encounter Books, an activity of Encounter for Culture and Education, Inc., a nonprofit, tax exempt corporation.

Encounter Books website address: www.encounterbooks.com

Manufactured in the United States and printed on acid-free paper.

The paper used in this publication meets the minimum requirements of ANSI/NISO Z39.48-1992 (R 1997)(Permanence of Paper).

FIRST EDITION

Library of Congress Cataloging-in-Publication Data

Bachiochi, Erika.
    The Cost of Choice: women evaluate the impact of abortion/ preface by Jean Bethke Elshtain ; edited by Erika Bachiochi.—1st ed.
        p.   cm.
    ISBN 1-59403-051-0 (alk. paper)
    1. Abortion—United States—Public opinion.   2. Public Opinion—United States.   I. Bachiochi, Erika.
HQ767.5.U5C66 2004
304.6'67—dc22
                                                    2004053210

10 9 8 7 6 5 4 3 2 1

For Dan,
Anna and Gabriella

Contents

Preface

JEAN BETHKE ELSHTAIN

A PREVALENT VIEW ABOUT CONTROVERSIAL Supreme Court decisions is that they hit the public unawares; there is an immediate hue and cry; then things settle down; eventually the holding is "normalized" and becomes part of the civic landscape. This is the story of *Brown v. Board of Education,* for example, the decision that declared *de jure* segregation unconstitutional. It would be unthinkable at this point—nearly a half-century after that decision—for any group to gain a hearing and garner support by calling for a reversal of the *Brown* decision. Even for those who believe that some of the remedies imposed by political bodies and courts in the aftermath of *Brown* were unwise, the holding that segregation violates the most enduring truths about America's commitment to moral and civic equality has indeed become part of the dense latticework of American civic and juridical life.

We are now more than thirty years on from the Supreme Court case of *Roe v. Wade,* but the controversy has not settled down. If anything, the issue is more unsettled than ever as, increasingly, slim majorities emerge to call for restraint and regulation of abortion. In other words, opposition to the extreme and radical nature of America's abortion order—embedded in *Roe* and, even more pointedly, in *Doe v. Bolton*—has not been "normalized" but, instead, has grown continuously since these decisions were handed down.

Why is this the case? One reason, surely, is that the abortion debate taps into centuries of reflection and argument on the moral status of persons. From the beginning of recorded moral philosophy, human beings have pondered and puzzled over the question of life itself and its moral status. We have measured progress in the West by our sometimes agonizingly slow movement toward recognition of the human status of those once denied such standing.

The history of slavery is a case in point. What was once routine in the ancient world—economies built on slavery—became, over time, problematic and, finally, unthinkable. It took many centuries, but eventually it came to pass. There was no moral justification—there could be no moral justification—for some human beings to enslave others. Movement toward women's moral and civic equality followed a similar path. The long arc that bends toward inclusion of human beings in the moral community rises from a recognition that the arbitrary removal of whole classes and categories of persons from moral concern—whether on the basis of race or gender or ethnicity or religion—is a sign of moral degeneration, not progress.

The question of the moral status of the unborn child is part of this long and arduous movement toward inclusion. Opponents of abortion insist that the unborn child belongs within the boundary of the moral community rather than outside it, excluded by judicial fiat. As Mary Ann Glendon points out in her contribution to this volume, most Americans do not realize just how "extreme the legal treatment of abortion is in the United States," and therefore do not appreciate that even Sweden, with its permissive attitudes toward human sexuality, "strictly regulates abortion after the eighteenth week of pregnancy." If they were aware of this, there would be even larger majorities calling for revision of *Roe* and *Doe,* and insisting on sturdy restraints upon what is currently a nearly unrestrained abortion right. We know this because all credible studies of public opinion demonstrate that majorities say they don't want *Roe* altogether reversed, but they also oppose permissive abortion at any stage of pregnancy or for any reason, and would allow it only for the most grave reasons having to do with incest, rape, or a serious threat to the mother's life. In other words, they do not believe abortion is, simply, a woman's "right."

In part, the form of moral recognition that is now bringing more people to the view that the moral status of unborn human life must be secured is driven by startling new developments in medicine. We can now *see* the unborn child as never before. No longer can anyone claim that that child is an invisible "it"; rather, the unborn human is some *body*. The assertion that the "fetus" deserves no moral concern because it is just an amorphous lump of flesh—"the product of conception," as the unborn child was named in radical feminist discourse and some legal argument in the 1970s—is no longer sustainable. Doctors can remove an unborn child from the womb, operate on this tiny full-fledged patient, tuck him or her back into the womb, and watch the fetus complete its development to the moment of birth.

A growing number of states and the federal government treat the intentional killing of an unborn child as homicide. The late Senator Daniel Patrick Moynihan, voting to prohibit the gruesome practice of so-called "partial-birth abortion," stated unequivocally that this procedure, one not recognized as a valid medical intervention by the American Medical Association, is so close to infanticide as to be indistinguishable from it. Overwhelmingly, the American public and majorities in the U.S. Congress agree. And yet . . . even though a bipartisan Congress passed and the President signed into law a ban of this procedure in 2003, it has been very difficult to bring about the popular will, given the ways in which *Roe* and *Doe* are judicially enshrined and sustained by certain ardent and well-financed interests. *The Cost of Choice* helps us to understand why. The story it tells is not a happy one.

Contributors to this volume explore what has been nearly taboo in discussion of abortion, namely, any negative effects on women themselves. In the radical feminist "pro-choice" literature of the 1970s and 1980s, the argument was that any woman who felt depressed or "let down" or regretful following an abortion was simply expressing "false consciousness." Her thinking had been so warped by "patriarchy" that she had "internalized her own oppression." This invited her to regret a necessary medical procedure that was no more significant than having a tooth pulled. I always found such arguments bitterly cruel . . . toward women. They diminished moral regret. They negated sadness. They downplayed conflict. Nobody at the time was discussing any possible negative medical or psychological consequences. It is high time the moral and medical questions, and the matter of negative consequences, are taken seriously as a contribution to taking women themselves seriously—which is supposed to be what feminism is all about.

My own background is that of a political theorist. I am trained to think politically and, politically, the decision of *Roe v. Wade* launched a civic debacle. Why is that? Because there was a political discourse concerning abortion going on in many states in 1973—all the messy processes of claim and counterclaim, negotiation and compromise—and the Court abruptly brought this process to a halt. The upshot I have already described: a civic and moral fissure in the body politic that will take many decades to heal, if, indeed, it ever will. The politics around this issue will be with us for a long time to come. The moral questions have always been there. That we can choose to ignore them does not mean anything has been resolved.

How, then, do we work our way back to a less extreme position than those encoded in the *Roe* and *Doe* cases? How does one speak about abortion in the wider context of American culture? For abortion, as I have already suggested, is not a narrowly legal matter: it is about who we are as a people and how we think about who is in and who is out of the moral community.

Is the unborn child inside or outside the circle of moral concern? That is the heart of the matter. Morally serious persons may differ on whether abortion should ever be permitted and, if so, under what circumstances; may clash on how best to talk about the moral value of the unborn. But no serious person can evade the question of who is inside or outside the circle of concern. Any treatment of abortion that does not face this question straight on is not serious and should be viewed as a form of propaganda and sophistry.

The Cost of Choice captures the moral, legal, medical and political complexity of abortion as a premise and as a practice. Agree or disagree as he or she will, the reader will surely concur that the *gravitas* that should attend any discussion of this painful issue is here displayed in full.

Introduction

MORE THAN THREE DECADES OF DEBATE about abortion has been largely a battle over rights—the reproductive rights of the woman, on the one hand, versus the rights of the unborn, on the other. In some sense, this long duel has sparked more heat than light, with rhetorical swords on both sides clanging over the same arguments, little new ground taken or lost, and each troop's own soldiers suffering battle fatigue. In another sense, however, the war has evolved and both camps have steadily gained ground for the perspective each has sought to emphasize.

Those who call themselves "pro-choice" have certainly consolidated an important position. Despite widespread moral opposition to abortion, approximately half of all Americans still hold a position that is "pro-choice," maintaining that whatever their personal beliefs, they do not have the "right to impose those beliefs" on anyone else. Abortion advocates have also had great success in convincing Americans that abortion is a necessary precondition for women's equality. To be against abortion is to risk being called anti-woman, according to the extraordinarily powerful dogma of our time brought about by the tireless efforts of abortion advocates.

Those who call themselves "pro-life" have likewise gained much ground for the central premise of the argument they have emphasized. Americans, on the whole, understand that a human life is taken by an abortion. A 1996 University of Virginia poll showed that only 16 percent considered abortion merely a "surgical procedure for removing tissue," the chosen description of many who advocate abortion. Meanwhile, three-quarters of those polled understood abortion to be the taking of a human life, with a large majority believing abortion to be murder. This is no small victory for abortion's opponents. No wonder they are confounded by the fact that this has not won them the war.

Abortion advocates have been hard pressed to answer the claim that abortion is the taking of a human life. The intellectually honest among them have simply conceded the point. For instance, pro-choice feminist Naomi Wolf admitted in a 1995 article in the *New Republic* that "the pro-life slogan, 'Abortion stops a beating heart,' is incontrovertibly true." Despite concessions of this kind, however, abortion advocates have continued almost unfettered to press the claim on which they have achieved the edge in the abortion debate: that whatever the status of the unborn, the very well-being of women is dependent on the legal right to abortion.

This collection of essays, written exclusively by women, is dedicated to examining this central pro-abortion claim. Though the twelve authors here do make a strong case against abortion, they do not do so by rehashing the now-familiar pro-life positions. Instead of emphasizing the human rights of the unborn, these authors focus on a theme more commonly linked with abortion advocates: that abortion impacts the well-being of women. However, unlike advocates of abortion, they do not see that impact as favorable. On the contrary, these authors argue that over the last three decades, legal abortion has had deleterious effects on women—socially, medically, psychologically and culturally. Putting aside the language of rights for now, the authors of the following essays analyze the nature of abortion's impact on women, looking to the historical record, medical fact and sociological reality. Their findings will be illuminating to those who consider abortion morally abhorrent but believe it is somehow good for women. These twelve essays compel us to rethink that once-sacred proposition.

• • •

THE COST OF CHOICE IS DIVIDED into three sections: Abortion, Women and Culture; Abortion and Women's Health; and Abortion, Law, Regulation and Alternatives. Mary Ann Glendon, Learned Hand Professor of Law at Harvard University, begins the first section by examining the cultural history and demographic changes that led to the Supreme Court's decisions in *Roe v. Wade,* and in *Roe*'s lesser-known companion case, *Doe v. Bolton.* Glendon contends that read together, these cases established an extremity in American abortion law unknown in any other liberal democracy— and perhaps unknown to much of the American public, which has never been fully informed of the decisions' scope and reach. Glendon maintains that the Court was emboldened to take such an extreme position on abortion because of the peculiar form of feminism that emerged in the 1970s, a feminism that has since become increasingly irrelevant to the lives of ordinary American women.

Candace Crandall, associate producer of the weekly PBS series *Think Tank* with Ben Wattenberg, further develops this historical examination through an assessment of abortion as the proffered solution to the social problems identified by the three great social movements of the 1960s and 1970s (civil rights, feminism, environmentalism). Crandall details the myriad ways in which legalized abortion has failed to provide the nation with great social benefit, instead helping to usher in social problems of its own.

Erika Bachiochi, a onetime "pro-choice" feminist activist, now a full-time mother of two, reflects upon the philosophical and legal characteristics of a culture consumed by "choice." Bachiochi describes how she came to challenge this cultural understanding in her own thinking and, as a consequence, began to view abortion as inherently antithetical to genuine feminism.

Serrin Foster, president of Feminists for Life of America, examines the curious course by which the feminists of the 1960s and 1970s abandoned the anti-abortion vision of their feminist foremothers to adopt a pro-abortion feminism that fails to really help women. Foster details how the nation can address the root causes of abortion and offer practical solutions.

Elizabeth Schiltz, mother of four and professor of law at St. Thomas Law School, describes the unsettling social reaction she experienced when she "chose" to carry to term a child with Down Syndrome. Schiltz then makes the case that society's widespread acceptance of genetic abortion has caused far too many to view individual human lives through the lens of a cost-benefit analysis in which some lives are deemed "unworthy of living."

Elizabeth Fox-Genovese concludes the section by arguing that legal abortion has been a "war on women." Calling upon the wealth of knowledge she possesses as the Eléonore Raoul Professor of the Humanities as well as professor of history and founding director of the Institute for Women's Studies at Emory University, Fox-Genovese casts great doubt on the often mentioned though scarcely analyzed refrain that "abortion helps women."

The second section, "Abortion and Women's Health," begins with an examination of the long-term health consequences women may face as a result of induced abortion. Dr. Elizabeth Shadigian, clinical associate professor of obstetrics and gynecology at the University of Michigan Medical School, reports that a history of induced abortion is associated with breast cancer, placenta previa, pre-term birth and maternal suicide. She calls upon professional medical organizations, governments and health agencies to fund long-term studies of women who have had elective abortions so as better to understand these and other potential health risks.

Dr. Angela Lanfranchi, surgical oncologist and assistant clinical professor of surgery at the Robert Wood Johnson Medical School, presents the epidemiological and physiological evidence supporting a link between induced abortion and an increased risk of breast cancer. Dr. Lanfranchi then takes on the arguments made against the link and explains why it has thus far been given scant attention by much of the medical community.

Dr. Joanne Angelo, psychiatrist and assistant clinical professor at Tufts Medical School, offers a moving account of how induced abortion has psychologically and spiritually affected the lives of real women. Bringing to bear nearly thirty years of experience as a clinical psychiatrist, Dr. Angelo discusses the importance of grieving to women who suffer after abortion.

The final part of the collection, "Abortion, Law, Regulation and Alternatives," opens with a thorough examination of the central abortion law decisions in *Roe v. Wade* and *Planned Parenthood v. Casey.* Attorney Paige Comstock Cunningham, senior fellow at the Center for Bioethics and Human Dignity, details the striking differences between the two Supreme Court decisions and indicates how the Court's abortion jurisprudence forsakes a true understanding of women and women's equality.

Attorney Denise Burke assesses the lax state of abortion regulation in the nation, offering evidence that contradicts the claim that legalizing abortion makes it safer for women. Burke contends that because abortion advocates oppose even the most standard medical regulations, present-day abortion procedures often rival the mythical "back alleys" of the pre-*Roe* era.

Dorinda Bordlee, an attorney who specializes in constitutional law in the field of bioethics, concludes the volume with an account of two legislative initiatives launched by states in an effort to promote life-giving alternatives to abortion. Bordlee explains how these initiatives respect the age-old truth that human fulfillment is found not through acts of self-assertion but through a "sincere gift of self." In contrast to pro-abortion policies that are based on a principle of radical autonomy, Bordlee maintains, these alternatives promote the inherent dignity and genuine uniqueness of all women.

Erika Bachiochi
May 2004
Norwood, Massachusetts

PART I
Abortion, Women and Culture

ONE

From Culture Wars to Building a Culture of Life[1]

MARY ANN GLENDON

WHEN *ROE V. WADE* CAME DOWN in January 1973, President Richard Nixon had just begun his second term and the nation was embroiled in the Vietnam War. Just around the corner, but unforeseen by any of us, were two momentous historical events: the fall of Saigon and the President's resignation. Something else that most of us did not perceive clearly at the time was that we were in the midst of a cultural revolution—a breakdown in traditional norms governing sexual behavior, accompanied by a sharp rise in family disruption that left an unprecedented proportion of the nation's children in fatherless homes and often in poverty. The social ecology of the country was being transformed, but this change came on so unexpectedly that it would be years before we took its full measure.

Even professional demographers were startled when they realized what had happened. Here is how Louis Roussel, head of the French National Institute for Demographic Studies, has summarized the transformation between 1965 and 1980:

> It is exceedingly rare in the history of populations that sudden changes appear across the entire set of demographic indicators. Yet in barely 15 years, starting in 1965, the birth rate and the marriage rate in all the industrialized countries tumbled, while divorces and births outside marriage increased rapidly. All those changes were substantial, with increases or decreases of more than 50 percent.[2]

By the end of the 1980s, those rates had stabilized at their new levels and people began to reflect on what all this might mean for the health and future of the country.

There has been a great deal of discussion about whether the changes that occurred in those years were good or bad for individuals, but until recently much less attention has been paid to what high rates of family breakdown and low birth rates will mean for the ability of the societies in question to produce the kind of citizens they need in order to sustain a healthy economy and a self-governing republic. One thing that can be said with certainty is that no society has yet adjusted to the consequences of the social upheaval just described—the loss of parental care and the looming problem of a labor force that is too small to provide for the needs of a large elderly population.

With hindsight, we can now see that *Roe v. Wade* and its companion case, *Doe v. Bolton,* came along just at a time when the United States (along with other affluent nations) was a few years into a massive social experiment. The better-known case, *Roe,* challenged an old Texas statute that banned abortion except when the mother's life was in danger. The other case, *Doe,* involved a more modern statute patterned on a draft produced by the prestigious American Law Institute. The statute in *Doe,* like many European statutes, permitted abortion but only under certain conditions and subjected it to regulation.

Though *Roe* got all the attention, it is fair to say that *Doe,* decided on the same day, was the more ominous of the two decisions. *Doe* was more ominous for two reasons that have never been well understood. First, by striking down a modern statute that attempted to protect both the woman's interests and the life of the unborn child, *Doe* signaled the doom of legislative efforts to provide even modest protection of unborn life. It was *Doe* that set the United States on a far more extreme course than that taken in most other liberal democracies, where the regulation of abortion has largely been left to be worked out through the ordinary democratic processes of bargaining, education, persuasion and voting.[3] (Even Sweden, the poster country for women's equality and liberal attitudes toward human sexuality, strictly regulates abortion after the eighteenth week of pregnancy.)[4]

Second, *Doe*'s broad definition of "health" spelled the doom of statutes designed to prevent the abortion late in pregnancy of children capable of surviving outside the mother's body unless the mother's health was in danger. By defining health as "well-being," *Doe* established a regime of abortion-on-demand for the entire nine months of pregnancy, something that American public opinion has never approved in any state, let alone nationally.

• • •

WHEN *ROE* AND *DOE* WERE GREETED in the legal world thirty years ago, what attracted the most attention were the separation of powers and federalism issues. The great constitutional lawyers of the day, like Paul Freund and Archibald Cox, were critical of the Court majority for striking down the statutes of all fifty states with so little warrant in constitutional text or precedent. Even Court watchers who favored legislative liberalization of abortion law were inclined to agree with dissenting Justice Byron White that the case represented an extraordinary judicial power grab.[5]

As for pro-life lawyers, most of them did not foresee how far the Supreme Court would extend *Roe* and *Doe* over the years—even to the point of striking down laws designed to protect late-term, healthy, viable babies. That is why, for years, the pro-life movement poured much of its energy into litigation, confident that *Roe* and *Doe* would eventually be limited, if not expressly overruled.

To be sure, there were a few who predicted where *Roe* would lead, but their fears were generally pooh-poohed. Who but a madman or a prophet would have imagined, as novelist Walker Percy did in *The Thanatos Syndrome*, that a whole industry of profitable "Qualitarian Centers" would spring up, where, as one of Percy's characters explains, doctors would respect "the right of an unwanted child not to have to endure a life of suffering."[6] Who but a madman or a prophet—or an artist who sees more deeply into things than the rest of us—would have imagined, as Percy did, that state governments might one day recognize a right to die, and that arrangements would be made for the sick and the elderly to push a button that would waft them away into a "happy death" in Michigan, a "joyful *exitus*" in New York, or a *"luanalu-hai"* in Hawaii?

• • •

IT IS SOMETHING OF A PUZZLE why the public has never really grasped how extreme the legal treatment of abortion is in the United States. Two factors combined to obscure the degree to which the U.S. has become careless about protecting human life at its fragile beginnings and endings. First, journalists and other opinion leaders—even Justice O'Connor in *The Majesty of the Law*[7]— have persisted in misdescribing *Roe v. Wade* as a case that permits abortion in the first trimester of pregnancy, but allows regulation thereafter. That was a flagrant misstatement of *Roe,* which permitted no regulation at all in the interest of protecting the unborn child for the first two trimesters. Moreover, when *Roe* is read with *Doe,* as the Court explicitly said it should be, third-trimester restrictions in favor of the child are effectively ruled out as well—for *Roe*'s dictum that such restrictions might be permissible if they do not interfere with the mother's health is negated by *Doe*'s definition of "health" as "well-being."

The second factor that enabled such radical decisions to pass beneath the radar is that most people just could not believe the Supreme Court would do such a thing. When I have described the extreme permissiveness of American abortion law to friends, one of the most common reactions is: "That can't be right." I have found that most people (including many law professors) have great difficulty wrapping their minds around the idea that the Court would permit the intentional destruction of a healthy infant who was capable of living outside his or her mother's body, when the mother's health (in the ordinary meaning of that word) is not in serious danger. That is why many of the same people who say they approve of *Roe v. Wade* also say they believe that abortion should not be permitted except for grave reasons, and that it should never be permitted after the fetus becomes viable except to save the mother's life.

What finally helped to raise public consciousness about these issues was one of the most shocking decisions thus far, *Stenberg v. Carhart,* where the Court in the year 2000 struck down a state statute that would have banned partial-birth abortion.[8] By that time, technology had advanced to the point where many parents were proudly displaying ultrasound photos of their babies at various stages of gestation. Thus, Justice Breyer's callousness in discussing something so close to infanticide highlighted as never before the discrepancy between the rigid, lethal logic of the Court majority and the more complex moral sentiments of most Americans.

If you read *Roe* and *Doe,* you may be surprised to see how little they have to say about protecting women, and how much they have to do with protecting doctors. That is because much of the pressure for these decisions came from the medical profession. Many people have forgotten that by 1973, with the sexual revolution well under way, licensed doctors were increasingly performing elective abortions for their patients. These doctors were quite worried about criminal and civil liability. Justice Blackmun, who had been counsel for the Mayo Clinic, wrote much of the *Roe* majority opinion in the clinic's library. He grounded the decision on a supposed constitutional "right to privacy" in the physician-patient relationship. It was not until years later that the Court majority went so far as to describe abortion as a woman's right, and not until 1992 that it shifted in *Casey* from the much-criticized privacy ground to treating abortion as a woman's individual liberty.

• • •

PART OF WHAT EMBOLDENED THE COURT majority to go as far as it did in the years when it was extending *Roe* and *Doe* was the embrace of abortion rights as a flagship cause by the peculiar form of feminism that took shape in the 1970s. To earlier feminists who had fought for the vote and for fair treatment in the workplace, it had seemed obvious that the ready availability of abortion would facilitate the sexual exploitation of women. Pioneering feminists like Susan B. Anthony and Elizabeth Cady Stanton regarded free love, abortion and easy divorce as disastrous for women and children. They would have regarded women who actively promoted those causes as duped or deranged.

But the feminism of the 1970s was different. What made it different was a puzzling combination of two things that do not ordinarily go together: anger against men and promiscuity; man-hating and man-chasing.

Around this time, some of my students began to ask me if I was a feminist. My answer, then and now, is yes—if that means I am specially concerned about a range of issues that disproportionately affect women. But as the mother of three young children in those days, I had to admit that I was baffled by the groups that were purporting to speak for women. As Professor Elizabeth Fox-Genovese has documented in her book *"Feminism Is Not the Story of My Life,"* organized feminism had almost nothing to say to women like me who were trying to juggle work and family obligations. In fact, many of its spokeswomen went out of their way to denigrate marriage and motherhood. Moreover, as a lawyer I could see that the chief beneficiaries of the divorce reforms they backed so enthusiastically were ex-husbands and second wives.

The feminism of the 1970s was decisively shaped by a demographic phenomenon that brought heartbreak and disappointment to two large groups of women and sent ripple effects throughout society. The first group was the cohort of women born in the early years of the post–World War II baby boom. These young women were caught in what demographers would later call the "marriage squeeze"—the shortage of potential mates that resulted from the sharp jump in birth rates.

In societies like ours where women customarily marry men one, two or three years older than themselves, a sudden spike in the birth rate will mean that there will be a shortage of mates in the usual age range for the girls born in the first few years of the surge. In other words, there simply were not enough boys born during the war years to provide husbands for the bumper crop of girls born in 1946 to 1949. The discrepancy was so great that there were 21 percent more girls born in those years than there were boys in the slightly older age group where those girls ordinarily would have expected to find husbands.[9]

It is interesting to think about when the effects of this demographic dirty trick would have begun to be felt: it would have been when these girls started dating in the early 1960s. Just imagine what a painful experience that must have been for young women who had grown up in the 1950s with magazines like *Ladies' Home Journal, Better Homes and Gardens* and *Good Housekeeping,* and had been socialized for domesticity. They had no idea why things were not working out the way they were supposed to.

The increased competition for mates, coinciding with the arrival of the birth control pill, helps to explain a number of things—such as the collapse of sexual taboos as young women began to pursue men more aggressively and to reach out toward men previously considered off-limits (such as other women's husbands). These changes affected nearly everyone, especially men, who took advantage of their suddenly dominant position in the mating market. Many women of Betty Friedan and Bella Abzug's generation found themselves alone and in difficult circumstances when their husbands divorced them to marry younger women. That created a second large group of angry women, and 1970s feminism was off to the races.

This pervasive sense of being wronged goes a long way to explain the otherwise incomprehensible willingness of many hard-line feminists to speak of abortion as a positive good, rather than as it is most commonly experienced by women: the tragic last resort of someone who feels frightened and abandoned.

The unusual conditions that gave rise to that particular form of feminism have long since passed, and thus it is hardly surprising that most women today are looking for something more responsive to their needs and aspirations. Betty Friedan, the smartest of the old guard, was the first of their number to see the writing on the wall. In 1996, in the *New Yorker*, she warned organized feminism that, "As a number of recent polls have made clear, the urgent concerns of women today are not gender issues but jobs and families." Two years later, in *Time* magazine, she again advised official feminism to get over its fixation on gender, saying, "All the sex stuff is stupid. The real problems have to do with women's lives and how you put together work and family."

Friedan was right that problems of work and family are central concerns of many women, and there are signs that she and others have succeeded in moving the feminist establishment to pay closer attention to that area. But hard-line feminism still has a tin ear for listening to women with children, as evidenced by the fact that their main proposal for solving the problem of combining work and family life is something that most mothers do not want: the socialization of child care. Ironically, the old feminism brought to light how much of women's work has been undervalued, but then bought into that very same disrespect by acting as though the only work that matters were market work. It is no wonder that four out of five young women today are so turned off by these negative attitudes toward men, marriage and motherhood that they reject even the term "feminism."[10]

It is now apparent to nearly everyone that what Betty Friedan calls the "sex stuff" does matter, and that it matters very much. As the bills for the sexual revolution pile up, it looks as though the feminists of the late nineteenth and early twentieth century were right on the mark. The price for the prolonged bacchanal of the 1960s, 1970s and 1980s has been high, especially for women and children. There's been a high cost in terms of women's health, including an epidemic of infertility caused by sexually transmitted infections, and a startling rise in cervical cancer among young women from the same cause.[11] The human papillomavirus is also apparently the cause of the recent appearance of oral cancers that previously were rarely seen in young women.[12] Where abortion is concerned, medical and psychological consequences abound.[13]

Most women have understood all along that *Roe v. Wade* would not, as Friedan once predicted, "make women whole." Leading polling organizations have consistently told us that a large majority of Americans, women even more than men, disapprove of the majority of abortions done in this country.[14] In recent years, that disapproval has increased significantly. A Zogby poll, reported in 2002, revealed not only that Americans in general are becoming more conservative in their views about abortion, but that young people are significantly more pro-life than their parents' generation were.[15] In fact, the most pro-life part of the population is people under thirty.[16]

• • •

WHY THEN, A CURIOUS PERSON MIGHT ASK, have those widely shared sentiments not tempered the extremism of American abortion law? It is probably, in part, because the Supreme Court has left so little room for the expression of popular will through legislation. It is probably also, in part, because so much confusion exists about what the law really says. But there are probably other, deeper reasons. With almost a million and a half abortions a year for thirty years, we have become a society where nearly everyone has been touched by abortion, if not personally, then through friends or family members. Anyone who speaks about abortion today is speaking to women who have had abortions; to men who have asked women to have abortions; to young people who have lost brothers and sisters to abortion, and to the mothers and fathers, friends and neighbors of those women and men. That knowledge often leaves us tongue-tied, at a loss for what to say and how to say it.

That knowledge has made it tempting to take refuge in slogans like: "Who am I to be judgmental?" and the famous "Personally, I'm opposed, but I can't impose my opinions on others."

I have to admit that back in the 1970s, I was rather uncritical of such phrases. I remember one day asking the dean at Boston College, a Jesuit priest, "Father, what do you think about this abortion issue?" He said, "Well you see, Mary Ann, it's very simple. According to Vatican II, abortion is 'an unspeakable moral crime.' But in a pluralistic democracy, we can't impose our moral views on other people." "Oh," I said. "OK."

I know this story reflects no credit on me, but it does show that many of us just did not focus on the issue all that closely. For one thing, I should have questioned the implicit assumption that the argument against abortion is only a religious argument. One of the great contributions of secular Jewish pro-lifers like Nat Hentoff has been to remind us of how dangerous it is for a society to become careless about protecting the lives of those who are weak, vulnerable, inconvenient or expensive to maintain.

I know, too, that I should have questioned the word "impose." But it took some time before growing numbers of Catholics, Protestants, Jews and persons of no religious faith stepped forward to point out that when people advance their moral viewpoints in the public square, they are not *im*posing anything on anyone. They are *pro*posing. That is what citizens do in a democracy—we propose, we give reasons, we vote.

It was only after I started to look into how controversial issues like abortion were handled in other liberal democracies, that I realized how unhealthy it is for democracy itself when the courts—without clear constitutional warrant—deprive citizens of the opportunity to have a say in setting the conditions under which we live, work and raise our children.

I should also have asked the dean why citizens should have to withhold their moral views on abortion, but not on other issues where he did not hesitate to advance a wide range of moral viewpoints—the Vietnam War, capital punishment, civil rights, relief of poverty. Years later, I did put a related question to the dean of the Harvard Law School. In the mid-1980s, after I had given a talk to the Harvard faculty comparing American abortion law unfavorably with the approaches taken in several other liberal democracies, the dean took me out for lunch and said, "You know, no one in that room agrees with you." Since he had put it in a friendly, avuncular kind of way, I asked him about something that had long puzzled me. I reminded him of how critical he and other constitutional lawyers had been of *Roe v. Wade.* "Why," I asked, "did you guys stop criticizing the even more extreme decisions that the Court handed down after *Roe?*" He sighed and gave me a spontaneous answer that had the ring of truth. "I suppose," he said, "it was because we had been made to understand that the abortion issue was so important to the women in our lives, and it just did not seem that important to most of us."

• • •

THIRTY-PLUS YEARS AFTER *ROE* AND *DOE,* the abortion issue is still more important to women than to men. But women and men alike are becoming more pro-life.[17] For one thing, in the age of ultrasound, we all have a clearer idea of exactly what is at stake. For another, many of the unintended consequences of the cultural revolution of which the abortion decisions were a part have come into clearer view. There is growing awareness that the moral ecology of the country has suffered something like an environmental disaster, and that we are faced with a very complicated cleanup operation.

What makes that task especially difficult now is that the social changes of the past four decades have taken a heavy toll on the nation's human capital. We now live in a culture where about half of all marriages end in divorce; where nearly half of all children spend part of their childhood in fatherless homes; where women and men who put their families first are falling behind economically and professionally; where many of the nation's youngest citizens are starving for parental time and attention, and often for basic material necessities.

Moreover, though hard-line feminism has little appeal for today's women, its ideology lives on in law and policy, like rays from a dead star. The cohort of women most captivated by that ideology now hold influential positions, and the organizations that advance the worst ideas of 1970s feminism continue to be handsomely bankrolled by its chief beneficiaries—the vast, profit-making abortion industry, the sex industry, and the organizations that promote aggressive population control.

Fortunately, however, the times are changing. There are many signs that new forms of feminism are emerging to tackle the challenge of renewing the culture. We are hearing more voices of women who are in touch with the real-life needs and aspirations of a broad range of women. We are hearing more voices of women who regard men and women as partners rather than antagonists in the eternal quest for better ways to love and work. We are hearing enough to give us hope that a great collaborative, creative effort is under way—an effort to promote a moral ecology that is in keeping with American traditions of welcoming the stranger, caring for the weak and vulnerable, lending a helping hand to the needy, and giving a fresh start to someone who got off on the wrong track.

TWO

Three Decades
of Empty Promises[1]

CANDACE C. CRANDALL

IN THE ARDUOUS FIGHT LEADING UP TO *Roe v. Wade*, the one thing feminists were most passionate about was their belief that unrestricted access to abortion was indispensable to achieving gender equality. Advocacy groups, including the National Organization for Women, the National Association for the Repeal of Abortion Laws (now NARAL Pro-Choice America) and the President's Advisory Council on the Status of Women, stood adamantly opposed to any limits, claiming that regulation would violate a woman's right to control her body.

When one looks at the data today, which reveal that half of all women undergoing abortion will be having at least their second and one of every five will be having at least a third abortion, a number of highly descriptive phrases come to mind.[2] "In control" is not one of them.

The successful push for unrestricted abortion on demand nationwide rested on two factors. The first was fortuitous timing. In the 1960s, the nation was caught up in the turmoil of three great social movements: civil rights, with its emphasis on bringing about sweeping political change via the courts; feminism, with its promise to empower the victims of very real social and economic injustice; and environmentalism, which had fostered widespread hysteria with warnings of an imminent population disaster. The point at which the tenets of these three movements converged was abortion.

The second and more important factor was packaging. From the outset, abortion was not so much a health issue as a political issue. And politics is personal. In 1968, public opinion polls indicated scant support for legalizing abortion; few Americans anticipated any personal benefit and many had serious moral concerns. But over the next five years, abortion rights advocates overcame such qualms with repeated assurances that when every child was a "wanted" child, broad social benefits would ensue.

According to this argument, illegitimacy would become a thing of the past. Women who found themselves inconveniently pregnant could obtain an abortion and remain in school or in the workforce. Couples would no longer be trapped into miserable forced marriages. Children would no longer be battered by parents resentful that they were "unplanned."

With its implied promise of reducing the need for welfare and social services for unplanned children and their mothers, abortion was transformed in the early 1970s from a moral question into a pocketbook issue. In 1971, a year after New York State legalized abortion, some New York politicians described the move as a significant step forward in dealing with the state's human problems. Members of the Commission on Population Growth, established by President Richard Nixon in 1970, thought so too. In the second of three reports, completed in March 1972, they called for Medicaid-funded abortions as necessary weapons in the "war on poverty," noting that "unwanted fertility is highest among those whose levels of education and income are lowest."[3]

This line of thinking already had support from *The Population Bomb,* the 1968 best-selling book by Paul Ehrlich, a biologist at Stanford. Ehrlich, who co-founded the group Zero Population Growth, warned that humans were rapidly populating themselves out of existence. Within slightly more than a decade, he predicted, all ocean life would die of DDT poisoning. Thousands would perish in smog disasters in New York and Los Angeles. Life expectancy in the United States would plunge to just forty-two years, as pollution-induced cancer epidemics decimated the population.

To much of the public, these forecasts seemed frighteningly plausible. Press reports told of earnest young college women having themselves surgically sterilized rather than risk bringing more children into an already overcrowded world.[4] In a controversial two-part episode of the popular CBS sitcom *Maude,* broadcast in 1972, the title character chose to have an abortion at age forty-seven, rather than become the aging mother of, as she put it, "an Eagle Scout."[5] News reports later revealed that the show had been inspired in part by a $5,000 prize offered by the Population Institute for the best prime-time script concerning population control.[6]

Abortion rights advocates, employing the rhetoric of equality, were quick to point out that wealthy women could always obtain a safe abortion, legal or not; so extending access to poor women simply corrected a social injustice. But the environmental scare presented a different sort of rationale: if all humanity was sitting on an increasingly overcrowded life raft, many reasoned, it might be unwise to let "the poor" occupy too big a corner.

By 1972, Americans were increasingly drawn to the banner of "choice." But did the nation benefit? Are women freer, happier, healthier?

Paul Ehrlich, a genuine expert on the Checkerspot butterfly, was not such an expert on human populations, as it turned out; his forecasts of impending catastrophe from overpopulation were never remotely realistic. Neither was the assumption that America could abort poverty out of existence. And illegitimacy, far from disappearing, has become a serious social problem. In 1970, the dawning of the age of abortion, just 10.7 percent of all births were to unmarried mothers.[7] By 1975, after *Roe,* the illegitimacy rate in the United States had jumped to 14.3 percent. Nearly 70 percent of black children and 33 percent of all children are born out of wedlock today.[8] Divorce rates have multiplied, as have reported incidences of child abuse.

What about the familiar refrain that abortion should be a matter between a woman and "her doctor," the so-called right to privacy? *Roe* hinged on this issue. The reality, today as in 1972, is that a woman's personal physician is unlikely to perform abortions. Two surveys—one by the American College of Obstetricians and Gynecologists in 1985,[9] the other by the Kaiser Family Foundation in 1995[10]—found that two-thirds of the obstetricians and gynecologists in practice in the United States, especially female doctors and those under forty, refuse to do abortions under any circumstances. Few of these mentioned public pressure from anti-abortion activists as a reason; most cited religious scruples or simply said they didn't like doing the procedure. Of the one-third who do perform abortions, a majority do four or fewer per month. That leaves most abortions to specialized clinics that offer women with unplanned pregnancies little in the way of counseling or emotional support.

Of course, the most powerful of the pro-choice arguments was that failure to legalize abortion would leave five to ten thousand women a year bleeding to death from coat-hanger abortions or dying from systemic infections incurred at the hands of "back-alley butchers."

Had anyone bothered to research that claim, then or since, they would have learned that every aspect of it was a myth. Death rates from infections and all types of surgeries, including illegal abortions, had already fallen precipitously after World War II, when antibiotics finally became available to the general public. But at no time—even before penicillin and sulfa drugs—had the number of abortion fatalities come anywhere close to the figure of five or ten thousand most often cited.

In 1940, the National Center for Health Statistics confirmed just 1,313 deaths as a result of illegal abortions, most of them due to infection. As antibiotics became available and surgical techniques improved generally, abortion-related deaths fell sharply: from 159 deaths in 1966, to 41 in 1972, the year before *Roe*.[11]

Confronted with these figures, abortion activists contend that most deaths were covered up. But if so, one would still have expected to see a dramatic decline in the overall death rate among women after 1973, when abortion became legal nationwide. According to Centers for Disease Control statistics, the death rate among women age fifteen to thirty-four, the group that today accounts for 94 percent of all abortions in the United States, saw no significant change in the years immediately after *Roe*.[12]

Nor were the abortionists of the 1950s and 1960s necessarily untrained. Dr. Mary Calderone, a former medical director for Planned Parenthood, estimated in the *American Journal of Public Health* in 1960 that nine out of ten illegal abortions were already being performed by licensed physicians.[13]

In this there is no little irony. Prior to *Roe v. Wade*, the fact
that these doctors were breaking the law kept the numbers of abortions relatively low—as few as 200,000 a year by some estimates—
and effectively discouraged most of the doctors from taking
unnecessary risks. Legalization removed that constraint. An
unscrupulous abortion doctor could now advertise openly, confident that he would be shielded by abortion rights rhetoric that
uniformly proclaimed him a hero, even if his motives were something other than compassion.

Only a year after abortion was legalized in New York State in
1970, writer Susan Edmiston noted with alarm in the *New York
Times Magazine* that state health department officials were failing
to supervise the numerous abortion clinics that had sprung up
throughout the city, establish accurate data collection, or take any
action on complaints that were already flooding in.[14] Reporters
were turning up similar problems in Los Angeles and the District
of Columbia. In 1974, the *Detroit Free Press* found unsafe, unlicensed abortion clinics proliferating in the Detroit area. In 1978,
a five-month investigation by the *Chicago Sun-Times* uncovered
dangerous medical practices at abortion clinics along Chicago's
Michigan Avenue.[15] In 1991, after several gruesome New York abortion cases made national headlines, the *New York Times,* in a front-
page article, found "filth" and "butchery" at dozens of shabby,
unlicensed clinics tucked away behind storefronts or—to evade
state regulators—operating out of ordinary-looking doctors' offices,
most often in poor neighborhoods.[16] But stories like these have
had essentially no practical consequences.

How much bad medicine is glossed over in the name of choice
is not known. It is regarded as politically incorrect for health agencies to keep good data on deaths and injuries at abortion clinics.
And since the much-publicized shootings at such clinics, newspa-
pers have shown a reluctance even to report any harm done by
the procedures they perform. But anyone can sit down at a computer, as I recently did, and pull up hundreds of newspaper
accounts documenting a long history of death, injury and fraud
at walk-in abortion clinics in Atlanta, Miami, Houston, St. Louis,
Boston, Chicago, Detroit, Kansas City, Birmingham, Los Angeles
and many other cities.[17] In this light, the commonplace references

to abortion as a "vital health service" and to attempts at regulating abortion clinics as "threats to women's safety" begin to ring hollow.

• • •

THE PAST DECADE HAS BEEN AN ESPECIALLY tough one for the abortion rights movement. Morale has visibly collapsed. In 1997 and then again in 2003, hard-fought and very public congressional debates over so-called partial-birth abortion—a procedure in which the physician partly delivers a late-term fetus feet first, then kills it by piercing its skull with scissors, attaching a high-powered suction device and sucking out its brain—revealed not only a disturbing brutality toward the unborn but also the widespread occurrence in this country of second- and third-trimester abortions. Facing a horrified public, which in 2003 acted through its political representatives to ban such procedures, abortion rights advocates remained ideologically rigid, stalling the enforcement of the federal ban through court injunction.[18]

With abortion becoming increasingly controversial and the vast majority of doctors reluctant to participate—and medical schools disinclined even to teach abortion techniques—advocates turned to RU-486 and other abortion-inducing drugs. But now, claims of a too-quick approval of RU-486 by the Food and Drug Administration and reports of deaths among seemingly healthy women who used the drug are raising alarms.[19] And this type of abortion—in which the dead embryo or fetus is passed in the toilet or the shower, with the woman herself as sole witness—may be even more emotionally traumatic than the various surgical procedures. Chemically induced abortions certainly do nothing to reassure the public that abortion is "humane."

Moreover, some who have been among abortion's most ardent supporters are now expressing doubts. Norma McCorvey, the "Jane Roe" of *Roe v. Wade,* defected in 1996 after being overcome by guilt at the sight of empty swings at a children's playground. Germaine Greer, though still holding tight to the feminist ideology she expressed in *The Female Eunuch* (1971), complained in her 1999 book *The Whole Woman* that abortion had become just one more oppression—this time by a male-dominated medical establishment that failed to inform women of the risks. She should know. By her own admission, several abortions left her sterile.[20]

For advocates of choice, surveys of public opinion have become more and more grim. A 1998 Wirthlin poll found that 58 percent of American women felt that the availability of abortion had hindered their relationships with men, and 70 percent of men and women believed that legal abortion was not necessary for women to pursue various educational and career goals.[21] A January 1999 survey of 275,811 incoming college freshmen by the Higher Education Research Institute showed that just 52.5 percent of men and 49.5 percent of women thought abortion should be legal—a decline of 14 percentage points since 1990 in an age group typically more pro-choice than any other.[22] In 2000, a *Los Angeles Times* poll indicated that just 43 percent of Americans supported a continuation of *Roe v. Wade,* down from 56 percent in 1991.[23] In the presidential race of 2000, while 27 percent of those polled by the *Los Angeles Times* said they were more likely to vote for George W. Bush because he was pro-life, just 18 percent said the same for Al Gore because he was pro-choice.[24]

Nationwide, the number of abortions has been dropping since 1990.[25] But a possibly more significant number was announced in February 2002 by the U.S. Census Bureau. Drawing on year 2000 data, the bureau reported that for the first time in three decades, the U.S. birth rate was up. Kids are no longer being regarded as a threat to the planet or as a woman's ball and chain. Where the two-child limit was once the hallmark of social responsibility, young couples are opting for more.[26]

• • •

INITIALLY HAILED AS A WOMAN'S TICKET out of the kitchen and into the boardroom, abortion today has become increasingly associated with sexual irresponsibility and cultural degradation. Once a proclamation of independence, a woman's admission that she has had an abortion has now become the kind of public announcement that makes men, and other women, cringe, regardless of their politics.

The ability of abortion to galvanize public opinion and tip the balance in favor of abortion rights candidates is over. Americans look at *Roe v. Wade* and increasingly find nothing in it for them. Should the opportunity arise, the nation may finally be ready to see the abortion issue returned to the state legislatures, where it should have remained some thirty years ago.

THREE

Coming of Age
in a Culture of Choice

ERIKA BACHIOCHI

I WAS BORN IN DECEMBER 1974, just about two years after the Supreme Court bestowed upon my sex what has become known as the "right to choose." Those who fought for the decision at the time and those who work diligently to maintain it today would undoubtedly argue that, indeed, I was born at possibly the best time in the course of history for a female to be born. After all, "the state's suppression of a woman's right to choose [was] simply a perpetuation of the patriarchal nature of our society. . . . To free women from [the] gender hierarchy, women must have a right to do what they please with their bodies." Therefore, a girl who grew up with the abortion right in her crown of jewels was one great step closer to true liberation from all that her mother and grandmother had suffered under the "patriarchy."

How do I know that this is what ardent "pro-choice" women think of this time in history? Because I was one of them. Indeed, the words I just quoted are my own, taken from an essay I wrote in college about eight years ago. The phrases "right to choose" and "the right to do what one pleases with her body" were expressions I used with some consistency early on in college as one of the leaders of our women's center. My use of such "pro-choice" rhetoric demonstrated that the culture of "choice" was *my* culture as I was growing up.

Before recounting how I grew out of this misunderstanding

of things, let me first reflect upon some of the primary character-
istics of the culture of "choice."

• • •

THE LEGALIZATION OF ABORTION three decades ago was
undoubtedly a catalyst in the development of what I am calling
the culture of choice; but this culture reigns in sectors of American life—and perhaps all of Western life—well beyond abortion.
Indeed, for the university elite and for the population at large,
"choice" has become the great human value, regarded as "the
foundation of moral obligation" in democratic society.[1]

The French political philosopher Pierre Manent defined the
centrality of choice in the Western moral imagination with this
axiom: "No individual can have an obligation to which he has
not consented."[2] In this way of thinking, all relationships—business or personal—find their basis for commitment in the contractual model, in which only parties who have consented, *and happily
continue to consent,* have obligations to one another. The contractual model works well in business relations, and is, importantly,
a basis of our free-market economy. It does not function so well
in the cultural sphere; indeed, it operates rather like a wrecking
crew upon marriage, family, and relations between a mother and
her unborn child.

In such a cultural mindset, obligation springs from choice,
and choice tends to follow the principle of pleasure or comfort.
Obligation is thus activated only when one *wants* to be obligated.
For instance, Americans on the whole are still likely to say it is
their spousal obligation to be faithful in marriage; yet the importance that some give to such fidelity diminishes greatly when they
no longer feel personally fulfilled in their marriage.[3] The ethic of
fidelity is then subordinated to the ethic of self-fulfillment—which
usually, as we know from divorce statistics as well as personal anec-
dote, wreaks havoc on children.[4]

The habit of choosing according to pleasure, as one does in
the cereal aisle, or according to comfort, as one might do in filing
divorce papers, tends to creep into the way we think about pregnancy and children too. Americans strongly insist that parents

must dutifully fulfill their obligations to their children; yet when a child is conceived by "accident" rather than by "choice," a large number of Americans—even when they know what actually happens in an abortion*—maintain that a mother should not be obligated to protect or care for a child in the womb. Why? Because they have bought into the philosophy pushed by the culture of choice: one is obligated only when one *wants* to be obligated.

To be sure, many Americans reject this attitude and adhere to more solidly grounded principles in their decisions and actions. Some may possess a pre-1960s, Kantian sense of duty for its own sake. Many others may hold a more religious understanding of moral obligation, in which virtues such as fidelity, justice, charity and and devotion to truth prevail over passions. These people understand that sometimes it is inconvenient, difficult, even self-sacrificial to do the right thing—and yet they do it. Increasingly, poll results reveal that a strong majority of Americans are uncomfortable with the current permissiveness in abortion regulation, favoring greater restrictions on its availability.† Still, the "choice" mentality has made inroads into the way many of us think about marriage, family and pregnancy.

The great irony in the culture of choice is that it actually promotes a malnourished kind of choice. Classically, it was understood that the will—that is, the choosing part of the person—had

---

*The Center for Survey Research at the University of Virginia reported in 1996 that 74 percent of Americans believed abortion to be the taking of human life. This included 38 percent who believed abortion to be murder, as bad as killing a person already born; 10 percent who believed abortion to be murder, but not as bad as killing a person already born; and 26 percent who believed abortion to be taking a human life, though not murder. Only 16 percent regarded abortion as a "surgical procedure for removing human tissue," while 11 percent had no opinion on the matter. See also James David Hunter, *Before the Shooting Begins* (New York: The Free Press, 1994).

†A 1999 CNN/*USA Today*/Gallup poll found that "16 percent of Americans think abortions should be illegal in all circumstances and 55 percent said it should be allowed only in cases of rape, incest or to save the life of the mother"; a 2001 Gallup poll found that 55 percent of Americans were in favor of "major restrictions on abortion" (i.e., legal in few or no cases); and a 2002 Zogby poll found that 25 percent favored a complete ban on abortion and 36 percent favored permitting it only in the cases of rape, incest or danger to the mother's life.

before it a variety of options and influencing passions; if the will was to maintain its freedom, it would choose among these with the guidance of intellect. A culture that truly honors freedom and the act of choosing, then, would be one that honors reason, the faculty that sorts through the various options and influencing passions, delving into the consequences for self and others of any one course of action, searching for the forces behind the stronger influencing passions, looking for possible external or internal coercive factors, and so on. Our contemporary version of choice, however, eclipses the governing role of reason, and so allows our passions to dictate the choices we make.

Abortion statistics reveal that this is the case. Most women have abortions out of fear, not as a reasoned response to the crisis pregnancy: they fear that they cannot afford to care for the child, that they are too immature, that they will be ridiculed, that they will be abandoned by their family or by the baby's father.[5] A culture that values the faculties of both intellect and will—that values the human person in the fullness of her dignity—would be one that comes to the assistance of the pregnant woman in crisis, helping her to see beyond her fears, to know of the help available to her, and to understand the nature of that which grows inside her. Such a culture would expect all educated people to have some understanding of fetal development and to value the dignity of the most innocent and helpless beings in the human race.

• • •

OUR CULTURE HAS SO ELEVATED the choices of will over reason that our laws support the notion that a pregnant woman can and should decide whether the fetus growing inside her is a person, in some cases protected by law, or merely the "product of conception," to be discarded at will. The "right to choose," as Professor Hadley Arkes of Amherst College puts it, has become "the right to decide just who is a human being, on the strength of my own beliefs, and as it suits my own interests. . . . Any evidence from embryology or genetics would be quite beside the point, for the decisive question is whether I myself regard the being as human."[6] While the law does not expressly state that any particular class of persons has a right to end the life of a person in any other class, the law *does* hold that a particular class of persons, pregnant women, has the right to decide whether those in another class, the unborn, are to be considered persons at all.

"Choice" has thus led to deep contradictions in law concerning the unborn. When a pregnant woman has decided to continue on with her pregnancy, more than half of American states recognize her *chosen* unborn child as a person in their homicide laws.[7] In Minnesota, for instance, a fetus at ten weeks gestation could be considered the victim of murder if intentionally killed by her *father*;[8] but if that same ten-week-old fetus is aborted by her *mother*, we call it women's liberation. Other states seek to ensure the health of the *chosen* fetus by protecting it from the mother's dangerous habits. In Baltimore, it was reported that a court took a pregnant drug abuser under its jurisdiction so she would not further harm the health of the fetus; yet that same woman, should she so choose, could legally end the life of the fetus with an abortion.[9]

Such legal contradictions illustrate why the language of the "right to choose" is so powerful and so deceptive. Pregnant women who have happily consented to that state for nine months know that were they to be assaulted and their baby killed as a result, they would expect their assailant to be punished. This is why contradictions in the law are not likely to be resolved by the dismantling of homicide laws that protect the unborn, as the most ardent pro-abortion advocates demand. For it is women who want these laws; and it would be an injustice to women—to mothers—to throw them by the wayside.

The power in the statement "right to choose" rests in some sense on this state of contradiction regarding the status of the unborn. It means not only the right to terminate a pregnancy, which in itself is a powerful right; as a matter of logic, it also gives the pregnant woman a prior, more powerful right that is deceptively unstated. That is the right to create one's own reality, to push aside reason and science in order to say—backed by the authority of the U.S. Supreme Court—"I will that this fetus is not a human being, is not endowed with the rights of a person, and therefore should not be protected by law."

Years later, that same woman, pregnant again but this time happily and consensually, has before her the right to choose again.

This time she says, "I will that this fetus growing inside me is a human person, and therefore (if I happen to live in a sympathetic state) endowed with the rights of a person and protected by law. Should any trauma befall this unborn child at the hands of another, the law must exact punishment. Should this child be born preterm at only a pound or two, the greatest minds in medicine should be brought to her care." These are the expectations held by pregnant women and mothers, and they are codified in various state laws by the people's representatives.

• • •

THREE DECADES AGO, THE SUPREME COURT initiated the idea that each individual pregnant woman, when it comes to the decision whether to abort, should act as her own philosopher, embryologist and judge concerning the humanity of the fetus inside her. More recently, in 1992, the Court enshrined this cherished notion. In *Planned Parenthood v. Casey,* a plurality of the Court wrote: "At the heart of liberty is the right to define one's own concept of existence, of meaning, of the universe, and of the mystery of human life. Beliefs about these matters could not define the attributes of personhood were they formed under compulsion of the State."[10]

Few would argue against the claim that each individual in a free society can, and indeed should, seek answers to the greatest human questions such as the mystery of human life. But to maintain that the criteria of personhood are to be defined by each individual's own concept of what constitutes human life goes well beyond the bounds of religious liberty or freedom of conscience—especially now that technology has given us the means to see inside the uterus.

The Court's philosophizing in *Casey* is reminiscent of an earlier time in our nation's history, a time of marked embarrassment to all American people, when individuals were permitted to determine for themselves whether those with black skin were human beings to be respected as such, or property to be used according to one's will. A judgment of this kind—who is to be considered a person—is far too important and fundamental to be left to personal interpretation. To do so is to elevate will over reason and crown Nietzsche king of American law and culture; it is to endorse a philosophical coup d'état of our experiment in ordered liberty.

• • •

THESE ARE WHAT I TAKE TO BE the basic markings of the culture of choice: It is a culture that employs a contractual, con-
sumerist mentality when it comes to marriage and family generally,
and pregnancy specifically. ("If I did not intend to get pregnant,
then I am not responsible for the care of my unborn child.") It
teaches that happiness depends on making choices according to
one's own desire or pleasure, or one's own (often fear-based) assessment of one's needs. The age-old notion that good character is
built upon good choices made in the midst of difficult circumstances has been replaced by indifference to attaining good character at all. Finally, and most frighteningly, the culture of choice
has exalted the impulses of human will and passions over truth
and reason. It is no wonder that so many are caught in its seduc-
tive trap.

I was very much caught in this trap. In preparing this essay,
I searched for stories from my teenage years and before in hopes
of detailing how I came to be a twenty-year-old college student
steeped in the culture of choice. Few anecdotes came to mind—
so few, indeed, that I began to see the truth about my story, and
perhaps those of other similarly situated young women. The simple matter was that I drank the water drawn from the tap of American culture. And there was no one around—no parent, no teacher,
no pastor, no mentor—to urge me to consider carefully that reality might be otherwise.

My support for abortion was not based on some experience
I had with a girlfriend in a sticky situation, nor was it the result
of indoctrination by a wildly pro-abortion mother. No, I was "pro-
choice" because I was a feminist. And I was a feminist because I
cared, and cared deeply, about women, about children, about the
poor in America and beyond. Where I went to college, feminists
were the ones who talked seriously about poor and needy women,
the ones who cared more about justice and social change than
about parties and fraternities. Feminists were the ones—at least
the only ones I had heard—who seemed to have suggestions for
how to address these concerns systematically.

The so-called "right to choose" simply went along with feminism. Reproductive freedom, the freedom to have a child only when one is ready and willing to have a child, was synonymous with women's rights. Women would never be equal to men unless abortion was available. After all, how could women attain the public status of men or achieve liberation from economic dependence on men if they had to tote around babies? How could women achieve all they wanted to professionally, all they were capable of doing with their new freedoms and opportunities, if they had to carry and then deliver an unexpected child? I do not mock these arguments; I once fully believed and asserted them.

That I came to change my mind about abortion, about feminism, and about the culture of choice generally is a rather lengthy and multifaceted story, with elements that are philosophical, religious, moral, psychological and political. External catalysts took the form of challenges by college professors, books and friends. Internally, I faced a deep unrest about these matters as I began to search for truth in other areas of my life.

The chief difficulty I first had with abortion concerned the role it played in the lives of poor women—or the role, it seemed to me, that women's groups like the National Organization for Women thought it should play. I had been studying in Washington, D.C., during a semester of my junior year and interning with a small think tank that assisted state legislatures in their efforts to reform welfare. As I became more and more immersed in the problems of the poor, especially poor women, I grew more and more disgusted with the argument put forth by abortion advocates that the availability of abortion would assist poor women on the road out of poverty. The thought that we, as a nation, would attempt to solve the problems of the poor by helping them rid themselves of their own children haunted me. It especially offended me that the poor were not among the membership of the elitist women's groups that supposedly spoke for them.

I remember feeling very alone as I thought through the question of abortion afresh. I knew that I could return to college, where I was pursuing a minor in women's studies, with new perspectives on economics and politics; but the prospect of returning to the women's center with newly agnostic views on abortion frightened me. Wavering on the issue of abortion was, one might say, unpopular. Still, my life, once dominated entirely by fears of what others might think, had slowly but persistently taken a broad turn away from such concerns. While others rushed for the bars in Georgetown, I sat for hours and hours on my dorm bed in D.C. and read—for the first time, in many instances—the founding documents of our nation, essays on political philosophy, and cases in constitutional law. I had gone to Washington a zealous activist; I came away a real student. It might sound grandiose, but it is true nonetheless that during that semester, I fell in love with the pursuit of truth.

Returning to Middlebury College the following autumn, I changed my major to political science (and dropped women's studies entirely) so that I could continue my study of political philosophy. That study, along with strong religious intuitions that had been growing within, caused an epiphany of sorts regarding the subject of truth. I came to consider what was true about me, about the physical and metaphysical makeup of the universe, about reality, to be more important than what I felt or wanted the truth to be. That is, truth and the findings of reason (and later, of faith) took on a value well above my reputation among friends and family and my desire for esteem and comfort. When I took this step, the culture of choice lost an adherent.

As the pursuit of truth replaced the pursuit of self, I began to realize that the same disgust I had felt in Washington about abortion among the poor could apply equally to abortion among the better-off. My support for abortion had really depended on a belief that abortion was necessary in women's struggle to achieve economic independence from men and to take their place as equals of men in the public sphere. Two points of clarity changed my thinking on this, and so my view on abortion too.

First, I came to understand that the beauty and strength of women lies in their desire to give of themselves for others; the beauty and strength of women resides in their concern for those less fortunate, the helpless, the weak. These were not attributes imposed upon women by men to keep us from achieving prestige in public offices and places of commerce. Rather, such feminine virtues have always, until quite recently, been understood as marks of true nobility in both women and men. For women to consider these qualities of little worth in comparison with the competitive qualities hailed in the public sphere is to turn against both women themselves and those whom women have traditionally served.

The goal of feminism was to give women voices and options. I am eternally grateful for the opportunities I have enjoyed as a result of that struggle. The hope of feminism was that the world would see all that women could do once freed from the traditional tracks laid down for them. In the second wave of feminism, abortion was thought to be a necessary—perhaps *the* necessary—choice on the way to achieving this. But instead, abortion hijacked feminism. Rather than elevate the status of the feminine virtues in the public sphere and teach the power of serving, as a true feminism ought, mainstream feminism, having allowed itself to be corrupted by the abortion imperative, taught women to place the ambitions and desires of the self above those in need, and to value power more than truth and love. Some women, persuaded by this corrupted feminism, have sacrificed their very womanliness—most manifest in the ability to bear a child—by having abortions in order to continue pursuing success in the public sphere. Such a course of action is inherently anti-woman and anti-feminist—and a source of contradiction in the feminist movement. The vast majority of Americans seem to agree: contrary to the claims of mainstream feminism, 70 percent of Americans do not think abortion is necessary for women to achieve educational and career goals.[11]

The second point of clarity I reached concerning these matters involves the great influence women have in the world through their efforts to serve the truth and to love others in the private sphere. As a result of the abortion culture's influence on how women think about themselves, the arenas where women traditionally found outlets for the service of others—home, schools, hospitals, local communities—have been neglected. And conversely, the decision to abort is more attractive to women in a culture like ours where women's work as mothers and caretakers is esteemed little. Hearts will not change concerning abortion until women, whether working in the public sphere or laboring in the private domain, insist through both words and deeds that acts of love are far more impressive, attractive and noble than acts of power.

As women—and men—continue in the long struggle to see the weakest human beings among us protected in law and respected for their inherent dignity, women must understand the great power we have to transform the culture when we *choose* to place the well-being of persons, especially children, above the pursuits of passion, self and power.

FOUR

The Feminist Case
<u>Against</u> Abortion[1]

SERRIN M. FOSTER

THE FEMINIST MOVEMENT WAS BORN more than two hundred years ago when Mary Wollstonecraft wrote *A Vindication of the Rights of Woman*. After decrying the sexual exploitation of women, Wollstonecraft condemned those who would "either destroy the embryo in the womb, or cast it off when born."[2] Shortly thereafter, abortion became illegal in Great Britain.

The now revered feminists of the nineteenth century were also strongly against abortion because of their belief in the worth of all human beings. Like many women in developing countries today, the early American feminists opposed abortion even though they were acutely aware of the damage done to women through almost constant childbearing. They opposed abortion despite knowing that half of all children born at that time died before the age of five. Moreover, the early feminists understood that—much like today—women resorted to abortion because they were abandoned or pressured by boyfriends, husbands or parents, and lacked financial resources to raise a child on their own. They knew that women had virtually no rights within the family or the political sphere. But they did not believe abortion was the answer.

Without known exception, the early American feminists condemned abortion in the strongest possible terms. In Susan B. Anthony's newspaper, *The Revolution*, abortion was described as "child murder," "infanticide" and "foeticide."[3] Elizabeth Cady Stanton, who in 1848 organized the first women's rights conven-

33

tion in Seneca Falls, New York, also classified abortion as a form of infanticide and said, "When you consider that women have been treated as property, it is degrading to women that we should treat our children as property to be disposed of as we see fit."[4]

Anti-abortion laws enacted in the latter half of the nineteenth century were the result of advocacy efforts by feminists who worked in an uneasy alliance with the male-dominated medical profession and the mainstream media. Ironically, the anti-abortion laws that early feminists worked so hard to establish in order to protect women and children were the very laws destroyed by the *Roe v. Wade* decision a hundred years later.

Present-Day Mainstream Feminism

In the 1960s, certain factions of the women's movement did a sharp about-face. With respect to abortion, the goals of the more recent women's movement, as led by the National Organization for Women (NOW), would have outraged the early feminists. That which Elizabeth Cady Stanton had called a "disgusting and degrading crime" has been heralded by Eleanor Smeal, former president of NOW and current president of the Fund for a Feminist Majority, as a "most fundamental right." In deep contrast to the words of the early feminists concerning abortion, NOW hailed the legalization of abortion as the "emancipation of women."

Betty Friedan, credited with reawakening feminism in the 1960s with her landmark book, *The Feminine Mystique,* did not even mention abortion in the book's first edition. It was not until 1966 that the National Organization for Women included abortion in its list of goals. Even then, abortion had a low priority. It is a man—abortion rights activist Larry Lader, still active today—who credits himself with guiding a reluctant Friedan, the first president of NOW, to make abortion a serious issue for the organization.[5] Lader had been working to repeal the anti-abortion laws based on concerns over population growth, but state legislators were horrified by his ideas. (Moreover, it was immigration and improved longevity that were fueling America's population growth—not reproduction, which in fact had declined dramatically.)[6]

Lader teamed up with a gynecologist, Dr. Bernard Nathanson, to co-found the National Association for the Repeal of Abortion Laws, the forerunner of today's NARAL Pro-Choice America. Lader suggested to the NOW leadership that all feminist demands (equal education, jobs, pay and so on) hinged on a woman's ability to control both her own body and procreation.[7] After all, he argued, employers did not want to pay for maternity benefits or lose productivity when a mother took time off to care for a newborn or a sick child. Lader thus convinced the NOW leadership that legalized abortion was the key to equality in the workplace.

Dr. Nathanson, who later became a pro-life activist, said that he and Lader were able to persuade Friedan that abortion was a civil rights issue, basing much of their argument on the claim that tens of thousands of women died from illegal abortions each year.[8] Nathanson later admitted that they had simply made up the numbers so as to secure support for the cause.[9]

Lader and Nathanson's strategy was highly effective. NOW has made the preservation of legal abortion its number one priority. Its literature repeatedly states that access to abortion is "the most fundamental right of women, without which all other rights are meaningless." With this drastic change of outlook, a highly visible faction of the women's movement abandoned the vision of the early feminists: a world where women would be accepted and respected *as women*.

Finding Real Solutions

There are now 1.3 million surgical abortions per year in the United States.[10] The Alan Guttmacher Institute (the research arm of Planned Parenthood) reports that women have abortions for two primary reasons: lack of financial resources and lack of emotional support.[11] Pro-life feminists, like the early American feminists, recognize that abortion is a symptom of, not a solution to, the continuing struggles women face in the workplace, at home and in society. Pro-life feminists, represented by such national organizations as Feminists for Life of America, seek to address root causes and promote solutions—from prevention to practical resources.

The first step in addressing the root causes of abortion is to empower young women and men to make life-affirming choices. No compassionate person, pro-choice or pro-life, wants to see a teenage girl drop out of school and face a lifetime of poverty because she became pregnant. No compassionate person wants her to suffer the pain and anguish of abortion.

Public and private funding for comprehensive programs that emphasize teen pregnancy prevention must be increased dramatically. Unbiased evaluation and replication of effective programs that include proven strategies, such as life-planning skills and mentoring, must be conducted.

Boys as well as girls should be included in the remedy. Groups like Feminists for Life and pregnancy resource centers regularly get calls from women who are pressured by partners who say they will pay $300 for an abortion but will not pay a dime in child support. Men and boys need to know that, thanks to laws that strengthen child support enforcement and paternity establishment, they can no longer coerce women into having abortions by threatening to abandon their children if they are born. But fathers need to do more than make payments. Their presence is needed in their children's lives. For women whose partners are absent and who are unable to support their children, assistance must come from both private and public sources and must provide the basics, including affordable, quality child care, and education and employment opportunities for the mother.

If we are serious as a nation about significantly reducing the number of abortions, then established, credible pregnancy resource centers should be eligible for federal funding. Nearly four thousand pregnancy care centers and maternity homes nationwide guide women in crisis through the maze of available support services—food, clothing, housing, furniture, medical care including high-risk pregnancies, legal assistance, help with employment and education, counseling for drug abuse and domestic violence, classes in childbirth, breastfeeding and parenting—all at no charge. Some specialize in bilingual/bicultural services, adoption and/or post-abortion counseling. These are the places where pro-life people "walk their talk" to help women in need. They leverage financial and in-kind resources from individuals, businesses, churches and communities across the country, yet they cannot consistently meet the demand for services without public financial support.

One model pregnancy care program is First Resort of California. Founder Shari Plunkett approached the HMO Kaiser Permanente with a plan to reduce the number of abortions in the San Francisco Bay Area. After thoroughly reviewing the program—even editing brochures—Kaiser agreed to refer clients who were unsure about having abortions to First Resort. As a result of the joint effort, Kaiser's client satisfaction rate was 99.3 percent. When NARAL's California affiliate succeeded in pressuring Kaiser to terminate the program, women lost the opportunity to make an *informed* choice.

Across the country, Americans on both sides of the abortion debate agree that women have a right to make informed decisions about their pregnancies. Women would be empowered to exercise this right by the passage of "Right to Know" legislation. As with any other medical procedure, women have a right to full disclosure of the nature of the abortion procedure, the risks and potential complications, and alternative support services, as well as the father's responsibilities. A woman has the right to know her doctor's name, whether he or she will be available if a medical emergency occurs, any history of malpractice or revocation of a medical license in any state; she has the right to a fully equipped clinic and/or ambulance nearby in case of complications, as well as the right to legal redress if she is hurt by the abortion.

Abortion clinics now have no uniform inspection or reporting requirements; even veterinary clinics are better regulated. Doctors who have botched abortions, caused infertility or death and lost their medical licenses have been known to jump state lines to continue performing abortions and even open new clinics.[12] There are no regulations to stop them.

Employers and educational institutions can also implement policies that ensure meaningful options for pregnant and parenting women (as well as parenting men). Women in the workplace should not have to choose between their child and their job; that is no choice at all. Employers who have not already done so should consider flex time, job sharing, on-site child care and telecommuting. Women need maternity coverage in health care; men and women need parental leave. Living wages would enable parents to support their children.

Similarly, women should not be forced to choose between their education and life plans and their children. As Feminists for Life has expanded its College Outreach Program in recent years, a number of college counselors have told us that the only choice they are aware of is between various abortion clinics—as if women were not capable of reading or thinking while they are pregnant or parenting. Feminists for Life is leading forums on college campuses that challenge university officials to provide housing, on-site child care, and maternity coverage within student health care plans, and to inform women about their hard-won right to child support. We have developed comprehensive Pregnancy Resources Kits with the input of those on both sides of the debate—including abortion doctors, pro-choice clinic staff, attorneys and students—to give women "the rest of the choices."

Feminists for Life has reached out to pro-choice activists to help provide more options for women, but ironically, Planned Parenthood, the nation's largest abortion provider, has characterized Feminists for Life's solution-oriented program as "anti-choice." If providing practical resources that help women can be called "anti-choice," something has gone terribly wrong. It is time to set aside the rhetoric and think again about how we can help women in need.

FIVE

Living in the
Shadow of Mönchberg
Prenatal Testing
and Genetic Abortion

ELIZABETH R. SCHILTZ

I WAS BORN AND RAISED IN GERMANY. My father was drafted into the U.S. Army during World War II and sent over to England with the U.S. Field Artillery, he fought his way through the D-Day invasion and the Ardennes, and was finally mustered out in Paris when the war ended. He stayed in Europe as a civilian working for the U.S. Army, providing logistical support for the American troops in Germany who arrived as occupation forces and eventually became NATO partners. Family legend has it that he used the free call given to all U.S. soldiers at the end of the war to call my mom in Pittsburgh and ask her to marry him and join him in Germany. I am not sure if this is true, but I do know that she did marry him and join him in Germany. That is where they lived until my father retired and they moved back to Pittsburgh.

My parents began their married lives as members of the occupation forces in an utterly defeated and devastated Germany. As part of the Marshall Plan, to get the German economy back on its feet, the Army subsidized the hiring of Germans to help the Americans as handymen, maids or nannies. One of the people that my parents employed to help with our rapidly growing family—I was the fifth of six children—was a woman named Theresa Böhm. Initially hired as a maid, she then became more of a nanny, and eventually a cherished unofficial member of our family. I knew her only as *Oma*—Grandma. She was our substitute grandmother, filling in for the ones living an ocean away from us. She was the one

39

whose musty little home we visited on holidays and in whose huge featherbed we snuggled on long visits during summer vacation.

That little house of hers, with that huge featherbed, was in a tiny village called Göbelnrod in the German province of Hessen. But that is not where Oma was born. She was born in the nearby town of Hadamar, which sits in the shadow of a tall hill called Mönchberg, or Monk's Mountain. On top of that hill stands an old Franciscan monastery, converted into a state hospital and nursing home in 1803.[1] In 1940, however, when Oma would have been just about the age I am right now, that hospital was turned into one of the infamous Nazi "killing centers." These were the six institutions spread all over Germany where initially children and then later also adults with disabilities such as, in the language of those times, "idiocy and mongolism (especially when associated with blindness and deafness); microcephaly; hydrocephaly; malformations of all kinds, especially of limbs, head, and spinal column; and paralysis, including spastic conditions"[2] were taken, systematically starved to death or gassed, and cremated.[3]

Oma rarely spoke to us about her experiences during the war, but we know that she was affected by the experience of living in the shadow of Mönchberg. All the accounts one reads about the Hadamar institute emphasize the heavy smoke from the crematorium chimneys, visible to the local inhabitants and horrid in smell.[4] One contemporary account of living with that smoke is found in a letter written in August 1941 by the Bishop of Limburg. He wrote, "The effect of the principles at work here is that children call each other names and say, 'You're crazy; you'll be sent to the baking oven in Hadamar.' ... You hear old folks say, 'Don't send me to a State hospital! When the feeble-minded have been finished off, the next useless eaters whose turn will come are the old people.'"[5] Oma was always terrified of hospitals. As she grew older, she had increasingly more emphatic conversations with my mother about not letting anyone take her to a hospital if she got sick. Sadly, she did end up dying in a hospital, though peacefully, at the age of eighty-three.

We know that living in the shadow of Mönchberg affected Oma in other ways, too. Although she loved all six of us kids very dearly, she had a favorite, and she never made even the feeblest attempt to hide it. The other five of us were all her *Silberfische*—silverfishes. My older brother, Jim, was her *Gelbfisch*—goldfish.

Jim was born mentally retarded, in 1952. At the time, the medical professionals counseled my parents to send him to live in an institution. They refused, and with much work and love, they taught Jim to do all those things the medical professionals said he would never do, like talk and walk. Jim graduated from high school. He is totally bilingual—fluent in both German and English. He reads the newspaper every day. He has held the same full-time position in the kitchen of a country club for twenty years now, and does not receive any sort of public assistance. Jim is known around our family as "the human jukebox" for his uncanny ability to remember the lyrics to any song, from any era, by any artist.

Oma doted on Jim. When he was a baby, she spent endless hours massaging his legs and encouraging him to walk—indeed, she was the first person in our family to see him actually walk on his own. Once Jim got to be six or seven years old, he would stay with Oma a couple of weeks every summer. One of the things she spent a lot of time doing was teaching him fine table manners. If he did something that didn't pass her strict standards of etiquette, she would admonish him, *"Wir sind hier bei vornehme Leute!"*—"We are in the company of distinguished people!" Oma was emphatic that Jim should take his place in society with "distinguished people," that nothing about his condition justified any sort of exclusion.

In some sense, although we did not live in the town of Hadamar, I think that all the kids in my family grew up in the shadow of Mönchberg as well. I cannot remember a time when I didn't know that the first targets of the Nazis' gas chambers were people with disabilities. I cannot remember a time when I didn't know that my brother Jim would probably not have been allowed to live if he had been born just ten years earlier, in the same hospital in Frankfurt where I was later born—a former German military hospital in which my mother, the first time she was there, noticed swastikas carved in the borders along the tops of the walls. I grew up with a visceral awareness of the potential within humanity to decide it is legitimate to kill certain categories of people because of the costs that their lives impose on society. I grew up loving a brother I knew was in one of the categories of humans that the Nazis had determined to possess a *lebensunwertes Leben*— a "life unworthy of life," whose cost to society exceeded its worth.[6]

But that was years ago and far away. I grew up, moved back to the United States for college, went to law school, then plunged into life as an all-American working mom, practicing law and raising kids in the modern, progressive metropolis of Minneapolis. And then something happened to change my life. In so many ways now, on so many days, I feel as though I am still living in the shadow of Mönchberg.

When I was about five months pregnant with my third child, Peter, I got a copy of this:

Patient: Schiltz, Elizabeth

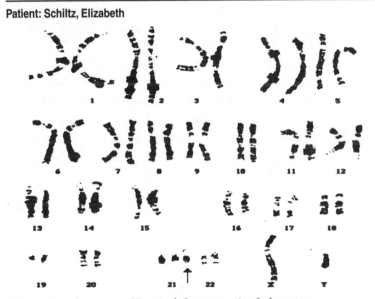

Abbott Northwestern Hospital Cytogenetics Laboratory

This is the karyotype of one of Petey's cells that was floating in amniotic fluid extracted from my womb by a big needle during a procedure called amniocentesis. The arrow in the karyotype points out that Petey's cells have *three,* rather than the usual two, copies of chromosome number 21. This indicates that he has an incurable chromosomal condition called Trisomy 21, or Down Syndrome, or, in the quaint, old-fashioned language of the Nazi regime, "mongolism."

The amniocentesis that my husband and I chose to undergo was the fourth in a series of prenatal tests we had performed during that pregnancy. The first was a blood test to assess the amount of "alpha-fetoprotein" (AFP) in my blood. That AFP test is routinely offered to women early in pregnancy, along with a slew of other tests. Every time you go to your doctor when you are pregnant, it seems, a nurse takes vials of blood to test for things like anemia, Rh factors, HIV—all conditions affecting the mother's health directly and the baby's health indirectly. Any responsible mother would want to take these tests to protect her health and that of her baby. With Petey, my AFP test showed a lower-than-normal amount of the alpha-fetoprotein, thus indicating a higher-than-normal statistical probability that the baby I was carrying had Down Syndrome. The probability based on my age alone was 1:378.[7] My AFP test results raised the odds to 1:170.

When my obstetrician shared these results with me, I chose to have another, more detailed blood test (the "triple screen," which tests three different substances), hoping that I would be reassured that nothing was wrong with the baby. In fact, this second test gave me odds of 1:38. Faced with that information, my husband and I decided to have a Level 2 ultrasound, a very detailed ultrasound that might detect indications of Down Syndrome, such as some of the heart or stomach abnormalities often associated with the condition. Although that ultrasound showed no signs of Down Syndrome, we chose to proceed with the amniocentesis that resulted in that karyotype.

The medical professionals I was dealing with through these four tests were not trying to find information to help me protect the health of my baby. Unlike anemia or HIV, there is little that can be done about the conditions that these tests were designed to identify. They were offered for the purpose of bestowing upon me a special societal privilege to choose to abort my baby. That karyotype could have been my ticket to a guilt-free, utterly justified, absolutely legal abortion—even five months into my pregnancy.[8] If the technology had existed in the 1940s, that karyotype would almost certainly have been Petey's ticket to Hadamar.

As someone who has always been pro-life, I did not accept these tests for the purpose of obtaining that "privilege." I just wanted to know, partly in the hope that I could be reassured that nothing was wrong, but also so that, if I could not be reassured, I could at least be prepared. I am a nerd. If I was going to have a baby with Down Syndrome, I wanted to read every book on the subject before the baby arrived.

Experiencing this testing sequence firsthand, however, gave me some insights into the potentially pernicious effects of the pre-natal testing process. The tests are all offered in the guise of "reassurance."[9] They all carry with them the implication that the responsible mother can and should do something constructive with the results: take extra iron if she is found to be anemic, take AZT if she has HIV, abort the baby if he has Down Syndrome. If you lack the financial or other resources to raise a child with a disability, you could easily be swayed by an argument that the knowledge you now possess about the child gives you the responsibility to do something constructive to solve the problem—by doing away with the child.

Now, this argument could obviously be a powerful incentive for a person to choose an abortion. Going through this process personally made me acutely aware of its power. But this was not the aspect of the experience that really *surprised* me. What surprised me was that people did not stop making this argument once I had rejected it during the testing phase. When I started telling people that the baby I was expecting would have Down Syndrome, colleagues asked me incredulously, "Why are you having this baby?" While there was something rather creepy about being asked that question directly, by someone staring at that big belly of mine while the baby kicked inside, it was still not so difficult for me to deal with. I was comfortable defending my position that I didn't believe in abortion, that I didn't think I had any choice in this matter; I was still in familiar, pro-life territory.

But I left that familiar territory the moment Petey was born, and I found, to my astonishment, that society still kept asking that question—why did you have this baby? I have seen people react with marked surprise when they hear that I knew Petey would have Down Syndrome before he was born. Though they do not ask aloud, you can see the question in their eyes: "If you knew, why did you have the baby?" What's buried in that question, deep in their eyes, is the perception of my son as a "choice"—specifically, *my* choice—rather than a unique human being created in God's image, a full-fledged member of the human race.

What I see in their eyes is the lingering shadow of Mönchberg that sometimes keeps me awake at night. I worry that the availability of abortion seems to be eroding societal consensus about our collective responsibility for vulnerable people—those with disabilities that were or could have been diagnosed prenatally, or even people born into difficult family situations or social structures. I am very frightened by the emerging attitude that if a woman exercises her "choice" to have a child who can be identified in advance as "vulnerable" for some reason, the woman herself bears full responsibility for dealing with that vulnerability.[10] In other words, if the "cost" of a certain life is going to be more than its "worth," someone has to make up the deficit. *If you "choose" to impose that cost on society by having a baby you could so easily have aborted, you should pay the price.*

Examples of this attitude abound. Bob Edwards, the scientist who created Great Britain's first *in vitro* fertilization baby, recently gave a speech at an international fertility conference in France in which he expressed just this view. He opined: "Soon it will be a sin of parents to have a child that carries the heavy burden of genetic disease. We are entering a world where we have to consider the quality of our children."[11] In other words, if we can identify a genetic condition before a child is born, and the parents choose to have the baby anyway, *they are committing a sin.* They're making a choice that society is going to have to pay for. *It is their choice—their sin. They should have to pay.*

Let me offer another example. A couple of years ago a woman's prenatal tests showed that her baby would have cystic fibrosis. When the baby was born, the HMO initially denied medical coverage because the baby had a "preexisting condition."[12] Although the HMO eventually reversed its decision, it first told the woman, in essence: *You knew about this condition before the baby* *was born. You could have prevented this baby from being born. You chose not to. Since you made that decision, you can find a way to pay for it.**

This same attitude lurks behind the increasing number of wrongful birth and wrongful life lawsuits being brought all over the United States.† In these suits, parents of children with disabilities (typically Down Syndrome) sue medical professionals for failing to diagnose the condition correctly before birth. The parents argue that they would have aborted the children, and thus "solved" the problem, if they had known about the condition. But since they were not given that option, they should not have to bear the costs; instead, the medical professionals who denied them their "choice" should pay. In other words, the "problem" is the fault of some identifiable person—in this case, a medical professional. That person, rather than society at large, should thus bear the cost.

This attitude is taking hold in other countries as well. In England, for example, a recent investigation found that doctors at one of the country's leading heart hospitals—the Royal Brompton Hospital—were discriminating against children with Down Syndrome. About half of all children with Down Syndrome are born with heart defects that can be fatal if not treated, but typically can

---

*A chilling example of similar reasoning is found in a recent law review article proposing to deal with the costs of raising children with disabilities by requiring all parents to pay a uniform per-child fee into a compulsory insurance plan. Parents who persist in bearing children with disabilities despite prenatal identification of the disability would be obligated to bear the cost of raising those children on their own, without assistance from the insurance fund. This article adopts the vocabulary, as well as the reasoning, of the Nazi eugenics programs; Part III of the article is entitled "Lives Not Worth Living." Erik Rakowski, "Who Should Pay for Bad Genes?" *California Law Review* 90 (2002): 1345.

†Wrongful birth cases are brought by parents arguing that the birth of a child with a disability caused harm to them by imposing on them the resultant burden of raising the child; wrongful life causes are brought by the person with a disability for damages resulting from being born with the disability. Legal causes of action for wrongful birth are recognized in twenty-two states; three states have rejected these suits. Kelly E. Rhinehart, "The Debate over Wrongful Birth and Wrongful Life," *Law and Psychology Review* 26 (2002): 141, 142. Legal causes of action for wrongful life are recognized in only three states (California, Washington and New Jersey). Ibid., 152. See also Jay Webber, "Better Off Dead?" *First Things* 123 (May 2002): 10.

be fixed relatively easily with surgery.[13] The inquiry did not find that the Brompton Hospital doctors were refusing to provide this lifesaving heart surgery to children with Down Syndrome, or that they failed to perform such surgery with all due care when they undertook it. However, the report did find that "in some cases there was a failure to provide a balanced view of all the options available to the families" of children with Down Syndrome. In consultations, parents of such children would essentially be told that the risks of the surgery were not worthwhile. Doctors "did not focus sufficiently on what was in the best interests of the child as the patient," but instead tended to stress the burden that the parents would face in caring for such a child.[14]

One of the most frightening aspects of this report is that it found that the doctors were not intentionally discriminating; they were acting in "good faith," honestly believing they were doing what was in the best interests of these families. They were acting on their professional belief that the cost of this lifesaving heart surgery was less justified for a child with Down Syndrome than for a child without it. In other words, the cost of saving the disabled child's life is not worth the burden that child would impose on society.

This same attitude also underlies the growing trend of creating designer babies by artificially fertilizing embryos and then conducting pre-implantation genetic screening in order to select only the embryos that lack certain problematic genes, or that have certain features, such as bone marrow tissue suitable for transplant to an ill sibling, or the desired sex.[15] Garland E. Allen, a historian of science, recently wrote an article in *Science* magazine comparing the social conditions that supported the spread of the eugenics movement in the early part of the twentieth century with the social conditions of today. He expressed a fear that they are the same, and he claimed, "As health care costs skyrocket, we are coming to accept a bottom-line, cost-benefit analysis of human life."[16] We can now create "perfect" babies. We can also abort less-than-perfect babies. *It is a matter of choice—your choice, Mom. If you choose to keep that less-than-perfect baby, that is your choice, but it is also your problem. You could have solved it for us. You chose not to. So you pay for that choice.*

Those who would adhere to a cost-benefit analysis of the lives of people with disabilities have to admit serious problems in determining how such a morally suspect analysis would ever work in practice. Some have attempted to calculate the *cost* of allowing a child with Down Syndrome to be born.[17] Although I am extremely skeptical of such calculations, I suppose, in theory, I could be convinced that a rough economic analysis *might* allow some generalizations, at least about the *financial* costs of raising a hypothetically typical child with Down Syndrome. But what possible criteria could be rationally imposed to quantify the *benefit* of such a life? Whose calculation of the benefit could one trust? Should we ask the people who really ought to know—people who live with disabilities? After all, disability rights activists maintain that "most people with disabilities rate their quality of life as much higher than other people think. People make the decision [to reject embryos] based on a prejudice that having a disability means having a low quality of life."[18]

Should we ask parents raising children with disabilities? *The Child Who Never Grew,* by Pulitzer and Nobel Prize winning author Pearl S. Buck, is a beautiful book about one such parent's experiences. Ms. Buck eloquently describes the heartbreak and sorrow she experienced in raising a daughter who was mentally retarded as a result of a metabolic condition called PKU (phenylketonuria). But she also describes some of the benefits:

> [B]y this most sorrowful way I was compelled to tread, I learned respect and reverence for every human mind. It was my child who taught me to understand so clearly that all people are equal in their humanity and that all have the same human rights. None is to be considered less, as a human being, than any other, and each must be given his place and his safety in the world. I might never have learned this in any other way. I might have gone on in the arrogance of my own intolerance for those less able than myself. My child taught me humanity.[19]

How can we possibly determine the market value of such lessons? What tuition would we charge for learning humanity?

Despite its methodological flaws, the "bottom-line, cost-benefit analysis of human life" clearly has become generally accepted in many spheres of our society. Can anything be done to dispel this dark and sinister shadow of Mönchberg's smoke cloud?

In the end, the cost-benefit attitude toward the lives of those with special vulnerability will have to be countered by an attitude that is deeper and stronger—and much more American. University of Georgia professor Edward Larson, winner of the 1998 Pulitzer Prize in history, authored a book in 1995 about the rise and fall of eugenic sterilization in the southern United States in the early part of the last century. In conclusion, he wrote: "At least in the Deep South, values founded on traditional religion and concern for individual rights served as more effective protection against the excesses of eugenics than did any internal regulatory mechanism within medicine or science."[20]

Values founded on the concern for individual rights, like the conviction articulated in our Declaration of Independence: "that all men are created equal, that they are endowed by their Creator with certain inalienable Rights, that among these are Life, Liberty and the pursuit of Happiness."

Values founded on traditional religion, like the statement from the Apostle Paul:

> The body is one and has many members, but all the members, so many though they are, are one body.... If the body were all eye, what would happen to our hearing? If it were all ear, what would happen to our smelling? As it is, God has set each member of the body in the place he wanted it to be. If all the members were alike, where would the body be? ... Even those members of the body which seem less important are in fact indispensable.[21]

These values are not empty platitudes. They are the foundations of our republic and our conception of democracy. These values must be forcefully asserted in each and every context in which anyone attempts, through a cost-benefit analysis, to adjudge any human life as not worthy of living.

SIX

Abortion:
A War on Women[1]

ELIZABETH FOX-GENOVESE

DURING THE WEEKS LEADING UP TO the thirtieth anniversary
of *Roe v. Wade,* there seemed to be more news and commentary
about abortion than there had been for years. The anniversary
always elicits a flurry of opinion, but 2003 was different, and not
only because of the significance of the anniversary. For one thing,
in President Bush we have a president who is pro-life not merely
for reasons of political discipline or expediency but, as far as one
can tell, for reasons of personal conviction—and faith. For another,
Republican majorities—however slim—prevail in both the House
and the Senate, and we will soon see one or more vacancies on
the Supreme Court, not to mention the many current vacancies
on other federal courts throughout the nation.

This new political configuration has emerged at a moment
when several major bills are pending before Congress or have
recently become law: the Born-Alive Infants Protection Act (signed
into law by President Bush in August 2002); the Partial-Birth Abortion Ban Act (twice vetoed by President Clinton, signed into law
by President Bush in November 2003); the Unborn Victims of Violence Act (signed into law by President Bush in April 2004); the
Child Custody Protection Act; the RU-486 Patient Health and
Safety Protection Act; and the Abortion Non-Discrimination Act.
Notwithstanding the cries of panic and outrage that met these
laws, none of them would threaten the core of *Roe v. Wade.* Presumably, the hyperbole of the pro-abortion forces derives in part

from their fear of the slippery slope: if you place any restrictions at all on access to abortion, you open the door to its recriminalization. But there is more to it than that.

The majority of Americans could live comfortably with the modest restrictions on abortion adopted by Congress. Until recently, most Americans apparently had only a vague impression of *Roe*'s provisions and assumed that it permitted first-trimester abortions but little more except in the case of unusual circumstances: rape, incest, or threat to the life of the mother. The pro-abortion lobby encouraged its supporters in their illusions, beginning with the claim that it was only defending a woman's right "to choose." Several developments of the last few years have nonetheless jeopardized that cultivated innocence.

The debates over partial-birth abortion have highlighted abortion's brutality and the possibility of performing it on babies who might otherwise have lived. On the other side, the growing sophistication and increased use of sonograms and ultrasounds have introduced innumerable couples to the human form of babies in the earliest stages of development. A mother who has seen a photograph of her "child" is less likely to turn to abortion than one who believes she is carrying only a bit of unformed "tissues"; moreover, a recent study shows that only five out of one hundred obstetrician/gynecologists are now willing to perform abortions.[2] These developments and many others have begun to shred the image of abortion as a "victimless crime," that is, no crime at all but only the fail-safe protection for a decent woman who wants to make the most of herself and her life.

The militancy of today's pro-abortion campaign is beginning to expose its real goals. At the heart of those goals lies a passionate commitment to the transformation of women's roles, their relations with others, and even their nature. Abortion advocates purpose a radical revision in what it means to be a woman—if not an abolition of the very substance and concept of woman. By now they have persuaded the media, who in turn have apparently persuaded most Americans, to replace "sex" with "gender," which the public now regards as more respectful of women's varied talents and capabilities. And most Americans agree that women deserve respect as persons "in their own right," which is to say as responsible and autonomous individuals. Most Americans—unless they or their children happen to have been exposed to women's studies, gender studies or cultural studies—probably do not understand the full significance of the displacement of sex by gender.

The theoretical rationales for the preference for gender may become dizzyingly convoluted, but they rest on the common premise that biology has betrayed and oppressed women, who must be liberated from it. First, proponents of gender argued that purported differences between the sexes were nothing but "socially constructed" gender roles, designed to keep women subordinate to men. That argument allowed for the possibility of a substratum of biological sex, but insisted that it was distorted by society's imposition of gender roles. More recently, cutting-edge academic theorists have dismissed sex entirely, arguing that the notion of a "real" biological sex is itself a sleight of hand—a trick of language employed to keep women in their place and to imprison the fluidity of everyone's polymorphous sexual desires. We may safely assume that most Americans do not fully grasp the connections that bind the preference for gender to the sanctity of a woman's unconditional right to abortion, but they include a commitment to a woman's right to liberation from her biological sex and especially from any children with which her body may betray her.

From the start, the pro-abortion forces have championed abortion as the cornerstone of women's freedom and have fought for its recognition as a fundamental right—the necessary precondition for women's equality with men. They have a point, albeit a deeply misguided one; and those who disagree cannot afford to underestimate its appeal. The pro-abortionists ground their case in a comprehensive worldview. Doubtless many of their followers either do not recognize the worldview or pay it little mind. But in some ways, their uncritical acceptance makes them all the more dangerous, for they do not understand the magnitude of what they are agreeing to. And their uncritical acceptance vastly strengthens the hand of the hardcore pro-abortion faithful, who understand precisely the magnitude of their blueprint for women.

How have the advocates of abortion convinced vast numbers of people, many of them decent people of good will, that women's prospects for happiness and self-realization depend upon unrestricted access to abortion? The simple answer lies in their success in convincing people that full personhood for women depends upon becoming truly equal to men—which effectively means securing freedom from their bodies and, especially, from children. The more complicated answer arises from the assumptions of our culture as a whole, especially its escalating sexual permissiveness, its loss of spiritual direction, its pathological fear of human mortality and the related cult of youth, its dedication to instant gratification and disdain for sacrifice, and, perhaps most portentously, its abandonment of children.

The more complicated answer contains key elements of the pro-abortion worldview. The defense of abortion grows logically out of a culture that is denigrating and eroding the ties that bind people together. This culture invites Pope John Paul II's label of "the culture of death," for it subordinates reverence for and joy in life to obsession with material goods and sexual desires. Ironies abound. The carriers of the culture of death fear and deny death, which they would forestall by any means imaginable: stem cell research, cloning, the harvesting of organs, and more. Their self-image as passionate defenders of life—their own and those of people like them—blinds them to the myriad ways in which they save one life at the price of another—often many others. In a small ceremony in the East Wing of the White House in September 2002, President Bush explained his opposition to embryonic stem cell research in words that echoed his State of the Union address of the previous January: "We must not create life to destroy life. Human beings are not research material to be used in a cruel and reckless experiment." By the same token, we must never destroy life to "save" another life—whether physically by providing organs or metaphorically by "liberating" a woman to complete an education or pursue a career or simply enjoy her "freedom."

Advocates of abortion try to square the circle by assigning the right of judgment to themselves: they will decide which lives are meaningful and which are not—which are real lives and which are not lives at all. A baby in the womb, conveniently dehumanized by the designation of "fetus," falls into the latter category, except when it is "chosen." As should be obvious, the standards that govern who is chosen can only be subjective and, consequently, reinforce the "me, me, me" tendencies of our times. Here we have another irony. The culture's emphasis on the autonomous or disconnected self serves many purposes, not least those of employers who seek to divest themselves of responsibility for as many benefits as possible and who have little or no patience with maternity leave.

The pro-abortionists' embrace of women's right to the anxious freedom of disconnected individualism has effectively deprived women of the protections and support that pregnancy and maternity require. Affluent women, who can afford unlimited paid help, may not suffer unduly from the practical inconveniences of individual liberation, but less-affluent women assuredly do. And most women suffer from the emotional disconnection. We now have a substantial number of depressing studies that demonstrate the high cost of abortion for women. We need not linger over the evidence of the many women dead from hasty, botched or unsanitary abortions, although we know there are enough to make one cry.[3] Predictably, the women who suffer are likely to be poor and often African American or Hispanic. As yet we lack reliable evidence about the number of these cases—but it may well exceed the highly dramatized number of pre-*Roe* back-alley abortions, which, according to Dr. Bernard Nathanson, was wildly inflated.*

We do, however, have studies that point to a link between abortion and breast cancer.[4] The precise nature of the link still provokes heated debate, but it is becoming increasingly difficult to dismiss its existence out of hand. Even the mainstream American media are now forced to acknowledge that a first pregnancy brought to term provides an important protection against breast cancer. By the same token, the interruption of a first pregnancy

---

*In his years as a pro-abortion activist, Dr. Nathanson maintained that 5,000–10,000 women died from illegal abortion each year; later he wrote, "I confess that I knew the figures were totally false.... But in the 'morality' of our revolution, it was a useful figure...." Bernard Nathanson, *Aborting America* (New York: Doubleday, 1979), 193.

may have potentially dangerous consequences, although a spontaneous miscarriage will not.[5]

The devastating emotional consequences of abortion are beginning to be even more widely documented. Women who have had abortions are at high risk for serious and lasting depression, and they are more likely than women who have not had abortions to suffer drug or alcohol addiction or even to commit suicide.[6] If women who have had an abortion subsequently have children, those children are more likely to experience a variety of emotional and behavioral problems than the children of women who have not had abortions—although appropriate psychological treatment that alleviates the woman's pain may ease her relations with the children who have "survived."[7] The majority of women who have abortions experience deep loss, grief and regret. Rather than liberate them, the experience imprisons them in pain. Doubtless we would benefit from more complete studies, but we now have enough evidence to say with confidence that for the vast majority of women, abortion represents a worst-case scenario—and, too often, a confirmation of their abandonment by the father of their child and by the larger community. More often than not, girls and women have abortions because they lack the support to have their child.[8]

Refinement of existing studies of abortion's impact should call attention to the social background of the women who have abortions: they are disproportionately poor. The response of middle-class academicians and activists is sadly predictable: Why should we be surprised if poor women—often women of color—manifest a variety of social pathologies? And how can we claim that the abortion "caused" such women's addiction or depression? But well-designed studies can correct for factors apart from abortion.

Meanwhile, we are left to wonder about the possible class and racial biases of the pro-abortion activists, who tend to be white and middle-class: What does it say about our society and our prospects for building a culture of life if privileged women encourage their least-privileged "sisters" to believe that they cannot bear the children they conceive? In the words of Damon Owens, national spokesman for Life Education and Resources Network (LEARN), "More black babies are killed in a three-day period by abortion than were ever lynched in the history of America."[9] Although estimates vary slightly, it is clear that abortions are now performed disproportionately on African American women as compared with white women. Thus while African Americans account for 12 percent of the population, African American women have 36 percent of the abortions.[10] Under these conditions, it is no wonder that sections of the African American community are beginning to respond with hurt and outrage—or even cry genocide. "Abortion is the number-one killer of blacks," said Rev. Johnny Hunter, LEARN's national director in North Carolina. "We're losing our people at the rate of 1,452 a day. That's just pure genocide.... The whole mindset Planned Parenthood has brought into the black community ... says it's okay to destroy your people. We bought into the lie."[11]

Before one dismisses that claim as hyperbole or hysteria, reflect upon the campaigns of Planned Parenthood, which still—however covertly and discreetly—solicits support by telling potential donors that they do not want to support "those" people's children; which supports offering birth control to even the youngest girls; and which passionately advocates the provision of abortion to the women of the third world. Cries of alarm about purported overpopulation inevitably—although again covertly—target nonwhite and non-Western peoples. And perhaps it should give us pause that among the most liberal abortion laws are those of England and Canada, both of which have national health services as well as high levels of immigration. Meanwhile, the flight from responsibility for children is resulting in a dramatic population decline in the developed world.

In addition to promoting a decrease in specific sections of the national and world populations, Planned Parenthood has been encouraging underage girls who engage in sexual relations with older men (a common pattern) to lie about their and their partners' ages in order to secure abortions without parental consent. This policy defies parental consent laws, frequently evades laws against the transportation of a minor across state lines, and amounts to nothing less than the aiding and abetting of statutory rape.[12]

All these strategies represent a concerted campaign to free women—and society at large—from responsibility for children.

According to the pro-abortion forces, women have for too long been saddled with a responsibility for children that has barred them from the most interesting and lucrative occupations—and often from any occupation at all. These charges contain enough truth to prevent our dismissing them out of hand. We gain nothing by denying difficult truths, and we risk trivializing our own case by doing so. Most women do want—and need—some regular interaction with the larger world and have much to contribute to it. Many women must earn some income if their families are to survive. The care that children need and deserve requires virtually as much time as most jobs and professions and is not compatible with them. If the past three decades have taught us anything, they have taught us that you cannot have it all—or, more accurately, you cannot have it all at once. Happily, for most people, life is long and permits women, like many men, one or more career changes. In addition, thanks to technological developments, the number of occupations that can be pursued on a part-time basis is growing, as is the number of opportunities for working from home. Yet the pro-abortion forces have attempted to resolve the contradiction between children and work by eliminating children from the equation—with disastrous consequences.

The temptations are great to find specific people to blame for the antisocial behavior or violent acts of children and adolescents. Easy targets include the parents who leave children in day care from seven in the morning until ten at night, or in the care of a "nanny" who may not really like children or her job or who may lack sufficient education to stimulate the development of a child's mind. And the whole country shudders at a Susan Smith, who drowns her own children, or at parents who leave their children locked in a house while they go off on vacation. But ascribing all the blame to particular individuals misses the point. The glorification of individual choice, epitomized in a woman's right to unrestricted abortion, has hardened our sensibilities even as it has cut children adrift to fend for themselves—often with results as chilling as those presciently described in 1954 by William Golding in *Lord of the Flies*.

At first glance, these problems may bear little relation to the harm that abortion inflicts upon women. Do not the demands of caring for children cripple women's freedom? Why should fathers not assume a full half of the responsibility, as proponents of "joint parenting" propose? Pro-abortion activists represent themselves as the last, best defenders of women's liberty. Without abortion, they argue, all of women's gains since the 1960s would be wiped away. On the basis of this logic, which the media promote, they claim the high ground of the true defense of women's interests. They have scored a remarkable rhetorical success, largely because of their political genius for appearing merely to express the received wisdom of "mainstream" culture. Where once Americans were enjoined to view women through the lens of "Mom and apple pie," they are now enjoined to see women through the lens of autonomy, power suit and briefcase. Countless Americans have been seduced into supporting abortion as the innocuous right to "choose" self-realization and fulfillment—no more than any self-respecting individual would ask. In this script, those who oppose abortion on demand—or any form of abortion at all—represent the forces of repression that seek to thwart women's development as persons and independent actors in the world.

If we are to challenge the logic of the pro-abortionists and the script to which it leads, we must first acknowledge the importance and justice of women's participation at all levels in the worlds of work, politics and the arts. We do not aspire to return women to subservient domesticity—much less to deprive the world of their considerable talents. Any such attempt to turn back the clock will fail, probably provoking destructive reactions along the way. The attempt will also impoverish any effort to defend the sanctity of life.

Our challenge is to turn the clock forward by offering women new visions that do not pit their lives against the lives of their children in a Darwinian struggle for survival. In that struggle, no one wins. Pro-abortionists consistently imply that the bearing and rearing of children is work fit for servants. And if many American adults have ignored their message, a distressingly large number of American children appear to have heard it loud and clear. They intuitively know, even if adults prefer not to, that the repudiation of children is the ultimate confession of moral and social bankruptcy. Even fewer people are willing to acknowledge that the repudiation of children is also a repudiation of women.

Not surprisingly, the most enthusiastic fans of abortion have been men—at least until they have children of their own. The availability of abortion liberates a man from the obligation to marry the woman he impregnates, although the chivalrous man usually offers to pay half the cost of the abortion. The pregnant woman does not always find the offer comforting. Middle-class women frequently bemoan the dearth of eligible men, never drawing the simple conclusion that the dearth may bear some relation to their own defense of their right to choose and, especially, their insistence that, because the baby is a mere extension of their sexuality, the decision is theirs alone.[13]

Not all women can bear children, and not all women wish to do so, but the potential to do so lies at the core of being a woman. Bearing children is what women can do and men cannot, and what makes perfect "equality" between the sexes a deceptive goal. By trivializing and even denigrating women's ability to bear children, legalized abortion has stripped women of their distinct dignity as women; it has shredded the primary tie among women of different classes, races, ethnicities and national origins; it has seriously diminished women's prospects for marriage and even further diminished their prospects for a lasting marriage; and it has exposed them to unprecedented levels of sexual exploitation. Welcome to the brave new world of freedom, ladies—and gentlemen.

Among the many horrors of the Holocaust, the most dangerous lay in the attribution to one person of the power to decide whether another should live or die. Even the slave system of the antebellum United States, which many evoke as an analogy for abortion, never granted masters such a power over slaves. That power severs the connection with, and recognition of, the other that, as Pope John Paul II has passionately argued, defines us as persons. Under the conditions of the Holocaust, the other became an object. The abortion culture allocates to a mother the power to decide that her own child is an object and authorizes her to do away with it. This opens the possibility for the richer or more powerful to measure all others—including the elderly, the handicapped and the seriously ill—in terms of their convenience and to dispatch those who fail the test, or whose care simply costs too much.

At the extreme, then, and dramatically in a world of managed—which increasingly means rationed—health care, abortion becomes the cutting edge of a war against our humanity. Throughout history, women have obtained abortions and committed infanticide, often because the men who impregnated them deserted them, sometimes through bad character or crass exploitation, sometimes because economic crisis conditions deprived them of the means to marry and support a family. But until our own time, these patterns have been cyclical, like the recurring wars that have deprived specific generations of women of the opportunity to marry. Our legalization of abortion and, yet more portentously, our proclamation of it as a positive good represents something new, and we should be rash indeed to expect it to go the way of previous cycles. Legalized abortion begins as a war against women, whom it tells that in order to be worthy, they must become like men. Perhaps worse, in severing the binding tie between women and the children they conceive, legalized abortion dismisses women from the company of responsible persons who are capable of sacrificing a piece of their freedom for the good of others—especially the children who embody our future.

The life issues, which begin with abortion, are emerging as the most important issues of our time, and women are their front-line custodians. It remains to be seen whether we will rise to the challenge.

PART II
Abortion and Women's Health

SEVEN

Reviewing the Evidence, Breaking the Silence
Long-Term Physical and Psychological Health Consequences of Induced Abortion[1]

ELIZABETH M. SHADIGIAN, MD

MOST OF THE MEDICAL LITERATURE published since the legalization of induced abortion has focused on short-term surgical complications, improvement of surgical techniques and training of abortion providers. The two commissioned studies that attempted to summarize the long-term consequences of induced abortion concluded only that future work should be undertaken to research such effects.[2]

Long-term complications are not well studied because of politics—specifically, the belief that studies of this kind would be used either to limit or to expand access to abortion. The political agenda of the researcher is questioned more in the study of induced abortion than in any other field of medical research. Many in the medical community fear that conclusions are too easily influenced by the author's beliefs about women's reproductive autonomy and the moral status of the unborn.

Approximately 25 percent of all pregnancies (between 1.2 and 1.6 million per year) are terminated in the United States; if there is even a small positive or negative effect of induced abortion on subsequent health, many women will be affected.[3] Therefore, despite the political stalemate within the medical community, research in this area is a central women's health concern.

Against the backdrop of politics there is also a serious epidemiological concern in this area: researchers can only observe the effects of women's reproductive *choices,* since women are not exposed to induced abortion by chance. Because investigators are deprived of the powerful tool of randomization to minimize bias in their findings, research must depend on well-done observational studies. Such studies rely on information from many countries and include legally mandated registers, hospital administrative data and clinic statistics, as well as voluntary reporting (or surveys) by abortion providers.

Nonetheless, given a few methodological caveats,* current research suggests that a history of induced abortion is associated with an increased long-term† risk of: 1) breast cancer; 2) placenta previa; 3) pre-term birth; 4) maternal suicide.‡

Breast Cancer

The four previously published systematic reviews of the literature[4] and two independent meta-analyses (one published[5] and one unpublished[6]) show that induced abortion causes an increased risk of breast cancer in two different ways.[7] First, when the first full-term pregnancy is delayed to a later time in a woman's life, the protective effect of a first full-term pregnancy is lost. Second, apart from the effect of this delay, induced abortion may separately (independently) increase the risk of breast cancer.

---

*The reader should note that: 1) limitations exist with observational research; 2) potential bias in reporting by women with medical conditions has been raised and refuted (see Chapter 8 in this volume); 3) the assumption is made that abortion is a distinct biological event (that is, the termination of pregnancy changes hormones dramatically, and therefore an aborted pregnancy cannot be counted as 20 percent of a normal, full-term pregnancy); 4) inconsistencies in choosing appropriate comparison groups exist; and 5) other possible confounding variables of studying abortion's effects over time also exist. J. M. Thorp, K. E. Hartmann and E. M. Shadigian, "Long-term physical and psychological health consequences of induced abortion: a review of the evidence," *Obstetrical and Gynecological Survey* 58:1 (2003).

†Long-term means manifesting more than two months after the procedure.

‡Induced abortion has been studied in relation to subsequent spontaneous abortion (miscarriage), ectopic pregnancy and infertility. No studies have shown an association between induced abortion and later spontaneous abortion. An increase in ectopic or tubal pregnancies was reported in only two out of nine international studies on the topic, while only two out of seven articles addressing possible subsequent infertility revealed any increased risk with induced abortion. Thorp et al. (2003), 40–48, 74–80.

The medical literature since the 1970s has shown that a full-term delivery early in one's reproductive life reduces the chance of subsequent breast cancer development.[8] This is called "the protective effect of a first full term pregnancy." This protective effect is illustrated in the table below, which uses the "Gail Equation" to predict the risk of breast cancer for an 18-year-old within a five-year period and also within a lifetime. The Gail Equation is used to help women in making decisions regarding breast cancer prevention measures. In the first scenario, the 18-year-old decides to terminate the pregnancy and has her first full-term pregnancy at age 32, as compared with the 18-year-old in the second example who delivers at term. The individual risk of these women is then assessed when the risk of breast cancer peaks. As the table shows, a woman's decision to have an abortion instead of a full-term pregnancy at age 18 can almost double her five-year and lifetime risk of breast cancer at age 50, regardless of race.[9]

Examples of the Loss of Protective Effect of a First Full-Term Pregnancy on the Risk of Breast Cancer[10]

All four women become pregnant at age 18. #1 and #3 abort their first pregnancy and deliver at 40 weeks in their next pregnancy at age 32. #2 and #4 continue their first pregnancy and deliver at 40 weeks at age 18.

Gail Variable	#1	#2	#3	#4
Race	Caucasian, Non-Black	Caucasian, Non-Black	Black	Black
Age	50	50	50	50
Menarche	12	12	12	12
Age first live birth	32	18	32	18
Number of first-degree relatives with breast cancer	0	0	0	0
Number of previous breast biopsies	0	0	0	0
Five-year breast cancer risk	1.3%	0.7%	0.8%	0.4%
Lifetime breast cancer risk	12.1%	6.5%	6.7%	3.6%

Abortion as an independent risk factor for breast cancer, apart from the delay of first full-term pregnancy, has been controversial because of the complexities in this type of epidemiological research. Many studies have shown no link between abortion and breast cancer risk, while numerous others have indicated such a link.

Four published review articles have been written to help further analyze these varied studies. Two of the reviews found no association between induced abortion and breast cancer,[11] while one paper found a "small to non-significant effect."[12] However, a 1996 meta-analysis* (by Brind et al.) reported an odds ratio (OR)† for breast cancer of 1.3 (or 95% CI=1.2, 1.4) in women with a previous induced abortion.[13] (An odds ratio of 1.3 means that for every ten women who developed breast cancer and had not had an abortion, 13 women who developed breast cancer had had an abortion.) One unpublished independent meta-analysis found the OR=1.21 (95% CI=1.00, 1.45).[14] A further finding of these two studies was that the risk of breast cancer is increased if the abortion is performed before a first full-term pregnancy. Brind et al. found an OR=1.4 (95% CI=1.2, 1.6), while the unpublished study showed an OR=1.27 (95% CI=1.09, 1.47). The two meta-analyses used different methodologies,[15] but reported nearly equivalent results that are statistically significant, and do show that induced abortion is an independent risk factor for breast cancer.‡

---

*A meta-analysis is a study that numerically combines data from several different sources (usually other published medical papers) to come up with a numerical conclusion that may or may not have the same conclusion as the aggregate of the individual papers. It is like a super-study of the other studies. Other review articles look at individual papers and report the results but do not numerically combine the data.

†The "odds ratio" (OR) of an event is the ratio of the probability of the event occurring, to the probability that the event does not occur. An OR equal to 1 (OR=1) indicates that there is no association with the disease. An OR greater than 1 indicates a positive association with the disease. An OR less than 1 indicates a negative association. Similarly, a "relative risk" (RR) greater than 1 is said to be a risk factor between an exposure and the end event. A "confidence interval" (CI) greater than 95%, where the numbers in question do not cross 1, is considered statistically significant and most likely not due to chance. In this paper, only statistically significant numbers are quoted.

‡A recent reanalysis of previously published studies was published in the *Lancet* as this volume went to press. Collaborative Group on Hormonal Factors in Breast Cancer, "Breast cancer and abortion: collaborative reanalysis of data from 53 epidemiological studies, including 83,000 women with breast cancer from 16 countries," *Lancet* 363 (2004): 1007–16. The author feels that a careful assessment of the limitations and strengths of the new study will be necessary to continue the ongoing analysis of induced abortion as an independent risk

In addition, the risk of breast cancer increases with induced abortion when: (a) the induced abortion precedes a first full-term pregnancy;[16] (b) the woman is a teenager; (c) the woman is over the age of 30;[17] (d) the pregnancy is terminated at more than 12 weeks gestation;[18] or (e) the woman has a family history of breast cancer.[19] *All* the pregnant teenagers in one study who had a family history of breast cancer *and* aborted their first pregnancy developed breast cancer.[20]

Placenta Previa

"Placenta previa" is a medical condition of pregnancy where the placenta covers the cervix, making a cesarean section medically necessary to deliver the child. In general, this condition puts women at higher risk, not just because surgery (the c-section) is necessary, but also because blood loss is greater and blood transfusions may be needed. Placenta previa also creates a higher risk of hysterectomy (the loss of the uterus), and therefore the need for more extensive surgery.

Three studies, each with over one hundred subjects, as well as one meta-analysis examined induced abortion and placenta previa. All found a positive association. Induced abortion increased the risk of placenta previa by approximately 50 percent.[21]

Pre-Term Birth ("PTB")

Twenty-four studies explored associations between abortion and pre-term birth (PTB) or low birth weight (a surrogate marker for pre-term birth) in subsequently delivered children. Twelve studies found an association that almost doubled the risk of pre-term

---

factor for breast cancer. Prior to the publication of the *Lancet* study, the National Cancer Institute and the American College of Obstetricians and Gynecologists published position statements saying that induced abortion is not an independent risk factor for breast cancer but did not sufficiently address the studies that do show such a link.

birth. Moreover, seven of the twelve identified a "dose response effect," which means a higher risk exists for women who have had more abortions.[22]

"Also notable is the increased risk of very early deliveries at 20–30 weeks (full-term is 40 weeks) after induced abortion, first noted by Wright, Campbell, and Beazley in 1972. Seven subsequent papers displayed this phenomenon of mid-pregnancy PTB associated with induced abortion. This is especially relevant as these infants are at high risk of death shortly after birth (morbidity and mortality), and society expends many resources [to care for them in the intensive care unit as well as for their long-term disabilities]. Of particular note are the three large cohort studies done in the 1990s, 20 to 30 years after abortion's legalization. Each shows elevated risk and a dose response effect. Because these studies were done so long after legalization, one would assume that the stigma of abortion that might contribute to under-reporting would have waned."[23]

Suicide

Two studies, one from Finland and one from the United States, have shown increased rates of suicide after induced abortion. The Finnish study reported an OR=3.1 (95% CI=1.6, 6.0) when women who had chosen induced abortion were compared with women in the general population. The odds ratio increased to 6.0 when women who chose induced abortion were compared with women completing a pregnancy. (In this instance, the odds ratio means that for every woman who had a baby at term who committed suicide, six women who had an abortion committed suicide during the same time period.)[24] The American study recently reported that suicide RR=2.5 (95% CI=1.1, 5.7) was more common after induced abortion and that deaths from all causes also increased RR=1.6 (95% CI= 1.3, 7.0) after abortion.[25] This finding was again confirmed in a separate 2004 Finnish study by the same author, which showed that the mortality rate after an induced abortion remains higher than for nonpregnant women RR=1.45 (95%=1.22,

1.73) and that pregnancy or birth reduces pregnancy-associated mortality RR=0.49 (95%=0.43, 0.56).[26]

In addition, self-harm is more common in women who have had induced abortion.[27] In England, psychiatric admission as a result of suicide attempts is three times more likely for women after induced abortion; but the same pattern does not hold for women prior to abortion.[28]

Maternal Mortality

Since there are no reporting requirements for abortion complications, including maternal mortality, on the national level in the United States, any statements made regarding the physical safety of abortion are based upon incomplete and inaccurate data. Though the Centers for Disease Control (CDC) began abortion surveillance in 1969, the CDC is not notified for more than 12 months in half of all maternal deaths, and many states are not mandated to report maternal deaths to CDC at all.[29] One study concluded that maternal deaths are grossly underreported: 19 previously unreported deaths associated with abortion were identified for the years 1979–1986.[30] The CDC officially maintains that for every 100,000 abortions there is approximately one maternal death (within 42 days of the procedure).[31]

Certain women are at much higher risk of death immediately after an induced abortion. For example, black women and other minorities have 2.5 times the chance of dying as white women, and abortions performed at more than 16 weeks gestation have 15 times the risk of maternal mortality as abortions at less than 12 weeks. Also, women over 40 years old have 3 times the chance of dying as teenagers.[32]

Deaths of women that occur within the year after pregnancy have recently been studied. These deaths, which include suicide and homicide, are regarded as pregnancy-associated. Three studies thus far indicate that suicide and death from all causes are higher among women who have had abortions than among women who have given birth.[33] However, the CDC does not currently count these pregnancy-associated deaths from suicide and homicide within one year after abortion in its tabulation of maternal deaths.

Conclusion

In its most recent edition of medical opinions, the American College of Obstetricians and Gynecologists inexplicably states:

> Long-term risks sometimes attributed to surgical abortion include potential effects on reproductive functions, cancer incidence, and psychological sequelae. *However, the medical literature, when carefully evaluated, clearly demonstrates no significant negative impact on any of these factors with surgical abortion.*[34]

The evidence presented in this chapter refutes ACOG's position. Women and their physicians look to ACOG for analysis of medical issues, but ACOG continues to publish factually incorrect statements about the absence of long-term risks from abortion.

Given the widespread utilization of elective abortion, the health consequences of the procedure are of profound importance to society. It is imperative for professional medical organizations, governments and health agencies to fund research that follows women who have had elective abortions through their lifetimes so as to document and quantify health risks. If properly conducted, this research will afford women and their health care providers a dramatic advance in knowledge—*regardless of the outcome of the studies.*

In the meantime, there is currently enough medical evidence to inform women about the long-term health consequences of induced abortion, specifically breast cancer, placenta previa, preterm birth and maternal suicide, as well as a higher rate of death in the year following abortion as compared with the year after childbirth and as compared with the general nonpregnant population. Women should also be informed of the inadequate manner in which maternal death is reported to the government, thus grossly underestimating the risk of death from abortion in both the long and the short term. Women deserve accurate medical information to help them in their medical decisions, and this includes informed consent for abortion. Doing anything less is a disservice to women, especially to women who may make or already have made difficult decisions concerning an unintended or crisis pregnancy.

EIGHT

The Abortion—
Breast Cancer Link
The Studies
and the Science

ANGELA LANFRANCHI, MD, FACS

WHEN *ROE V. WADE* WAS DECIDED more than thirty years ago, I was a third-year medical student at Georgetown University. In the third year, medical students leave the classroom and go into hospitals to do their clinical rotations. During those rotations, I found that *Roe* had had an immediate effect on the practice and ethics of medicine.

No longer would my obstetrics professor tell his students that his was a unique specialty with two patients to consider, mother and child. After *Roe,* we treated two patients only when the mother *wanted* the child. When the mother did not want the child, no consideration would be given to the humanity of the unborn. There was no longer a child but merely a blob of tissue, a "product of conception," a parasitic entity or whatever the mother chose to call "it." After *Roe,* every doctor in every state could legally take the life of a human being. On my pediatric rotation that year, I helped to resuscitate a child who was born prematurely—crying aloud, struggling to breathe. She was the result of a failed abortion. She was wizened and burned from the hypertonic saline used to try to abort her on the hospital floor just below the nursery. I can still see her clearly in my mind's eye.

A year and a half after *Roe,* I came to discover that something else quite profound had happened. The Hippocratic Oath, which had stood medicine in good stead for 2,400 years, had been changed. No longer would doctors swear never to "give a woman an abortive remedy," as we had over the centuries. After *Roe,* that portion of the oath was removed.

Ten years after *Roe,* I watched my mother fight and lose her battle with breast cancer. In addition to her physical torment, she suffered mental anguish at the thought of leaving my youngest brother before he was fully grown.

Twenty years after *Roe,* I was settled into a surgical practice devoted to patients with breast cancer. I found that the breast cancer risk was no longer 1 out of 12 women, as I had learned in medical school, but had increased dramatically to 1 out of 8. Furthermore, I learned that the women suffering from breast cancer were no longer only postmenopausal grandmothers but also thirty-year-old mothers of toddlers. I knew from my own mother's painful experience what they would face.

Breast cancer is the only major cancer that has continued rising. Most of this increase has occurred in members of my own generation, those women who were twenty to forty years old when *Roe* was decided. It has been estimated that an additional ten thousand cases of breast cancer occur each year as a result of abortion.[1] Thirty percent of my breast cancer patients who are in their thirties do not have a family history of breast cancer, but *have* had an induced abortion.

Published epidemiological studies, the physiology of the breast, and experimental studies conducted in mammals all evince a link between abortion and breast cancer—called the ABC link. Despite the evidence revealing such a link, many have tried to dismiss it with poorly conducted studies and flawed arguments. As a result of the politics surrounding abortion, organized medicine has, for the most part, failed to acknowledge the ABC link.

Public knowledge of abortion as a risk factor for breast cancer will not only help women to obtain truly informed consent; it will also help women who have had an abortion. Once a woman knows she may be at higher risk for breast cancer, she can take the necessary steps to increase the likelihood of staying well by early screening and risk reduction strategies.* Basic medical ethics requires that all women be given this vital information.

———————

*Screening increases a breast cancer patient's survival by detecting smaller cancers that are less likely to have metastasized. Smaller tumors are more curable

The ABC Link

Epidemiological Studies

Epidemiological studies support the abortion–breast cancer link. These studies, however, can never be taken as conclusive proof that any risk found is causal. For example, large studies would probably show unequivocally that more people with lung cancer carry matches in their pockets than those without lung cancer. However, this would not mean that matches cause lung cancer, even though large studies were done well, statistically significant and reproducible. Of course, it is biology that shows us that the carcinogens in cigarette smoke actually cause lung cancer. Similarly, without the support of the well-known breast physiology and experimental data, the epidemiological studies supporting the ABC link would be inconclusive.

Epidemiologists have developed the following six criteria to analyze risk. Each criterion must largely be satisfied before a risk factor can be considered a potential *causal* risk (rather than simply an association in the way that carrying matches and lung cancer are associated).

The patient must be exposed to the risk before the cancer develops.

One would think this criterion so obvious as not to require much discussion. However, the Melbye study, often referred to as the Danish study and considered flawless by those who deny the ABC link, violates this most basic criterion, as I will discuss below.[2]

There must be similar findings in many studies.

In other words, one or two studies are never conclusive evidence

---

because they are usually more differentiated. At present, mammography screenings start at age 40. As it takes an average of eight years for one cancer cell to form a mass of cells a half-inch in diameter, screening should start around eight years after an abortion. A patient who is 16 years at the time of her abortion should be screened by age 24. Screening methods need to be developed for these young women as the sensitivity of mammography is low for young, dense breasts. Women could also lower risk by avoiding hormones such as birth control pills and hormone replacement therapy. Lifestyle and dietary changes could also reduce risk. See also A. Lanfranchi and J. Brind, "Breast cancer risks and prevention," Breast Cancer Prevention Institute, 2002.

of a causal risk. In the case of the ABC link, 29 out of 41 world-wide studies reveal such a link; of studies conducted in the United States, 13 out of 16 show such evidence.

There must be statistically significant increases in risk.
Scientists must show with 95 percent certainty that the results in their studies could not have occurred by chance alone. There are 17 statistically significant studies that show a link between abortion and breast cancer, 8 of which were conducted in the United States.[3]

There should be a dose effect, that is, the risk should become higher with more exposure to the risk.
In the case of the causal link between cigarette smoking and lung cancer, for instance, the more cigarettes one smokes, the greater the risk of lung cancer. In the case of abortion, the longer one is pregnant before the abortion, the higher the risk of breast cancer.[4] But unlike the risk of cigarettes, where tens of thousands need to be smoked to increase risk, only one abortion can give a woman a life-threatening disease.

There should be a large effect observed.
In the case of abortion and breast cancer, there are subsets of women at very high risk. For example, in the 1994 Daling study, *every* teenager who had an abortion before the age of 18 *and* had a family history of breast cancer developed breast cancer by the age of 45. The study thus indicated that the risk could not be calculated and was reported as infinity (∞), that is, incalculably high.[5]

There should be a plausible biologic mechanism.
There is a well-established and well-described literature on breast physiology that can account for the abortion–breast cancer link.

Physiology of the Breast
The physiology of the breast provides the strongest evidence of the causal link between abortion and breast cancer. The same biology that accounts for 90 percent of all risk factors for breast cancer accounts for the ABC link. Simply stated, the biology rests on two principles.

The more estrogen a woman is exposed to in her lifetime, the higher her risk for breast cancer.

It is well established that estrogen is implicated in the formation of three cancers: uterine, germ cell and breast.[6] Estrogen can induce cancers to form in two ways: as a mitogen and as a genotoxin. A mitogen causes cells to proliferate, that is, to multiply through division (mitosis). Each time a cell divides to form two cells, it must replicate its DNA. During replication, copying errors and chromosomal rearrangements can occur, causing abnormal cells to form. These abnormal cells can be mutations or cancer cells. A genotoxin directly damages the DNA, initiating a process that causes the formation of cancer cells. Metabolites of estrogen have been shown to cause mutations.[7] Estrogen is so potent it is measured in parts per trillion.

If a woman starts her menstrual cycle early, at age nine for instance, and continues to menstruate into her late fifties, she is at higher risk for breast cancer, as she has been exposed to monthly estrogen elevations for a long period of time. This too is the science behind a recent, well-publicized study showing that the estrogen-based hormone replacement therapy increases the risk of breast cancer.[8] In a similar way, birth control pills can elevate breast cancer risk.[9]

The earlier a woman's breasts develop from immature Type 1 and 2 lobules to mature Type 3 and 4 lobules (see diagrams), the lower her risk of breast cancer.[10]

Type 1 and 2 lobules are known to be where cancers arise. Type 1 lobules are also referred to as the TDLUs (terminal ductal lobular units),[11] where ductal cancers arise. Ductal cancer accounts for 80 percent of all breast cancers. Type 3 and 4 lobules are mature and resistant to carcinogens. When a female child is born, she has only a small number of primitive Type 1 lobules. At puberty, when estrogen levels rise, the breast forms Type 2 lobules. It is only through the hormonal environment and length of a full-term (40 weeks) pregnancy that there is complete maturation of Type 3 and 4 lobules in the breast. This maturation protects a woman and lowers her risk of breast cancer.

This is why women who undergo full-term pregnancies have lower risk of breast cancer and women who remain childless have

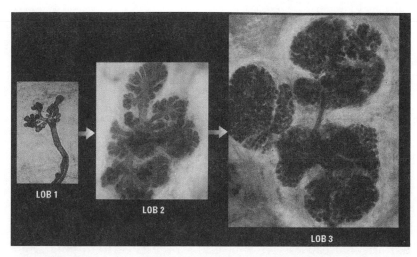

Figure 1: Human breast lobules at different stages of development. Immature lobules type 1 (LOB 1) and type 2 (LOB 2) (left and middle panels) are cancer-susceptible; the more mature lobule type 3 (LOB 3) (right panel) is cancer-resistant. *

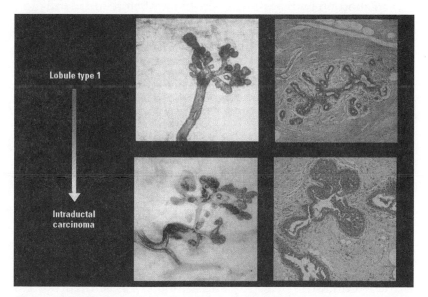

Figure 2: Comparison of a normal human LOB 1 (top panels) with intraductal carcinoma arising in the same structure (lower panels).†

---

*Whole mount preparation, toluidine blue stain (LOB 1, 2 and 3: x99, x118 and x121, respectively).

†Whole mounts stained with toluidine blue, histological sections with hematoxylin and eosin.

higher risk of breast cancer. Women who first give birth after age 30 are also at increased risk of breast cancer as their immature Type 1 and 2 lobules are exposed to estrogen for the many years from the time of their first menstruation until their first full-term pregnancy. Abortion in women under 18 and over 30 years old carries the greatest risk: these women have the highest percentage of Type 1 lobules in their breasts.[12]

It is the interplay of these two principles, estrogen exposure and breast lobule maturation, that accounts for the fact that abortion can cause breast cancer. Within a few days after conception, a woman's estrogen level rises. By the end of the first trimester, estrogen levels have increased by 2,000 percent. The estrogen stimulation that causes sore and tender breasts early in pregnancy results in the multiplication of Type 1 and 2 lobules. It is only after 32 weeks that a woman's breasts stop growing larger and mature into Type 3 and 4 lobules in preparation for breastfeeding.

If abortion ends a woman's pregnancy before full maturation of her breasts, she is left with an increased number of the immature Type 1 and 2 lobules. She now has a greater number of the breast lobules where cancers can arise, and this puts her at greater risk for breast cancer. It is through this same biologic mechanism that *any* premature birth before 32 weeks more than doubles breast cancer risk.[13]

Induced abortion thus increases breast cancer risk by three mechanisms. First, pregnancy exposes the breasts to high levels of estrogen for some weeks or months, which stimulates cellular multiplication. This increases the likelihood that an abnormal (or mutated) cell will form or be stimulated to grow into a malignant tumor. Second, the higher level of carcinogenic estrogen metabolites increases the rate of mutations, creating abnormal and potentially cancerous cells. Finally, abortion leaves the breasts with increased numbers of Type 1 and 2 lobules, since their normal maturation to Type 3 and 4 lobules in the last weeks of pregnancy is prevented. A woman who has an abortion then not only loses the protective effect of a full-term pregnancy by not developing these cancer-resistant Type 3 and 4 lobules; but because the pregnancy itself has caused her breasts to form an increased number of Type 1 and 2 lobules where cancers can arise, and then the abortion prevents the breasts from developing fully mature, cancer-resistant lobules, she is at greater risk for breast cancer than had she not become pregnant in the first place.

It is important to note that first-trimester spontaneous abortions (i.e., miscarriages) in general are associated with low estrogen levels and therefore do not cause an increase in breast cancer risk. A low estrogen level in these early miscarriages is the reason why the women will often say they had not even realized that they were pregnant. Because their estrogen levels never rose, their breasts never got sore or tender, nor did they experience any of the other symptoms of early pregnancy, such as morning sickness. This physiology is why it is vitally important that epidemiological studies differentiate between spontaneous first-trimester abortions (where women have not experienced increased estrogen levels) and induced abortions (where, assuming a hormonally normal pregnancy, estrogen levels have increased sharply).

Experimental Studies Performed in Other Mammals

Experimental studies performed in rats over twenty years ago support this biology. Rats that were given abortions had a 77 percent chance of developing breast cancer when administered the carcinogen DMBA.[14] None of the rats that had borne a litter of pups prior to receiving DMBA developed breast cancer; these rats enjoyed the protective effect of a full-term pregnancy.[15]

Arguments Made Against the ABC Link

Recall Bias

Recall bias is the most widely and oft-reported argument used to refute the ABC link. Recall bias is the hypothesis that women who have developed breast cancer will be more likely to admit that they have had abortions than women who are well. The theory is based on the assumption that healthy women are more inclined to conceal what could be embarrassing behavior, but are more likely to tell the truth should they become ill, seeking a reason for their illness.

Case-control studies in which researchers rely on interviews for their data are thought to be potentially susceptible to recall bias. Researchers assume that interviewees will not admit to "socially unacceptable behavior," such as abortion—unless they are sick. However, recall bias has not posed any such problem in other areas of medical research, where case-control studies have been used to gather data on other socially unacceptable behavior. For instance, in studies testing for a link between alcohol consumption and liver damage, interviewees were assumed to report their alcohol consumption accurately, whether or not they were sick. The same is true for interviews in which subjects were asked how many sexual partners they had, in studies on cervical cancer, and whether they were involved in anal intercourse, in studies on HIV. Abortion would not seem to be a more socially unacceptable act than any of these, yet recall bias is said to taint research about abortion though not the other behaviors.

Recall bias is a hypothesis worth testing; yet studies that have confirmed the ABC link controlled internally for recall bias in their study populations.[16] Moreover, although one study conducted specifically to test for recall bias in abortion–breast cancer research reported having found evidence of it, methodological problems were acknowledged after publication, revealing that the study actually failed to show that recall bias taints such research. Instead, the results supported what is true to clinical experience: almost equal numbers of women with cancer and without cancer concealed their abortions.*

---

*B. M. Lindefors-Harris et al., "Response bias in a case-control study: analysis utilizing comparative data concerning legal abortions and two independent Swedish studies," *American Journal of Epidemiology* 134 (1991): 1003–8. Researchers in the Lindefors-Harris study had before them both cancer and abortion computer registries in order to verify the responses of the women interviewed. Two groups of women were interviewed: those with cancer and those without cancer. The researchers hypothesized that more of those without cancer would deny their abortions than those with cancer. Such a result would be evidence of recall bias. Instead, they found no statistically significant difference between the responses of the two groups of women. Those with cancer and those without cancer underreported their abortions in approximately equal numbers (20.8 percent and 27.2 percent, respectively); that is, most healthy women and most sick women admitted to the abortions officially documented in the abortion registry, while some healthy women and some

The Melbye Study[17]

Another argument used against the ABC link is that there is one large and purportedly flawless study that provides a refutation of all the studies that confirm the ABC link. In a study of induced abortions between 1973 and 1992, published in 1997, Melbye et al. wrote in their conclusions that women who had induced abortions had no increased risk of breast cancer. Directly contradicting this stated conclusion, however, the abstract of the article notes that induced abortions beyond 12 weeks gestation led to a 38 percent overall increase in risk. Moreover, according to the study, induced abortions beyond 18 weeks gestation carried an 89 percent increase in risk. Apart from these contradictions in reporting, several other methodological flaws make the conclusions of the Melbye study suspect.

First, the study claimed that in Denmark, where it was conducted, abortion was legalized in 1973, when in fact abortion had been legal, though more strictly regulated, since 1939.[18] As a result of this error, 60,000 women who had had abortions between 1939 and 1973 were misclassified—that is, listed as not having had abortions which they actually had. These were among the oldest women in the study, and thus those most likely to have developed breast cancer. The exclusion of these 60,000 women from the data pool skewed the results of the study, lowering the relative risk of abortion reported by the researchers.

---

sick women lied. However, researchers did find that there were women—both healthy and sick—who admitted to having had abortions that were not documented in the computer registry. The researchers labeled this phenomenon "overreporting," claiming that women who told the researchers that they had had abortions that had not been reported in the registry were mistaken or lying (instead of assuming a mistake in the registry). Only with this wrong-headed assumption of overreporting did the authors then conclude that they had significant evidence of recall bias. Overreporting, of course, does not exist. The researchers were forced to acknowledge their error through letters to the editor in subsequent published correspondence. O. Meirik, H. O. Adami, G. Eklund. "Letter re: Relation between induced abortion and breast cancer," *Journal of Epidemiology and Community Health* 52 (1998): 209; J. Brind et al., "Reply to letter re: Relation between induced abortion and breast cancer," *Journal of Epidemiology and Community Health* 52 (1998): 209-11. Since most doctors read only the abstract of the paper and do not follow letters to the editor, a false impression of the study's results remains.

Another factor that contributed to the methodological flaws in this study has its basis in the biology of breast cancer. It takes an average of eight years for a cancer cell to grow into a clinically detectable cancer of a half-inch diameter. If an abortion in an 18-year-old causes a breast cancer cell to form, it is not likely to be detectable until she is at least 26 years old. Fully one-quarter of the patients in the Melbye study were under 25 years old when the study ended, accounting for only eight cases of breast cancer. Because of what is known about the development of breast cancer, these young women should not have been included in the study at all.

The most egregious of the Melbye study's flaws was the violation of the most basic criterion needed for a valid study: the risk, abortion, must precede the development of the disease, breast cancer. Therefore, a valid study would start collecting abortion cases before breast cancer cases. Melbye et al. did just the opposite. The researchers began tracking breast cancer in 1968, five years before they began tracking abortion, in 1973. In other words, all the abortion data on patients diagnosed between 1968 and 1973 who had had legal abortions before 1973 was simply missing, resulting in a misclassification of patients for these five years.

Despite these serious methodological errors, the Melbye study still found a statistically significant increased risk of breast cancer with second-trimester abortions. The risk increased 3 percent for each week of gestation before the abortion, revealing further evidence of both the biology and the dose effect of the risk of abortion. The longer a woman is pregnant before an abortion, the more Type 1 and 2 lobules she develops during the proliferation phase of her breasts, and therefore the higher her risk.

The Collaborative Group on Hormonal Factors in Breast Cancer[19]

In March 2004, the *Lancet* published a study hailed by its researchers, Valerie Beral et al., as the definitive analysis that puts to rest the claim that abortion increases breast cancer risk. The *Atlanta Journal-Constitution* quoted Beral as saying, "Scientifically, this is really a full analysis of the current data."[20] A review of the study, however, reveals that it is not actually a "full analysis." Indeed, serious methodological flaws—especially in the selection of studies to be included—renders the Beral et al. study unreliable.

Beral et al. made several errors in choosing the studies that made up their analysis. First, the researchers threw out 11 studies for unscientific reasons (e.g., "principal investigators could not be found," or "researchers declined to take part in collaboration"), and 4 other studies' worth of data were simply not mentioned at all.[21] Thus, they included only 24 of the 41 studies that show data on induced abortion and breast cancer from 1957 to the present. To supplement these 24 studies, the researchers also included 28 unpublished studies. This means that the majority of the studies included in their analysis had not stood the test of peer review.

A closer look reveals that many of the statistically significant studies that show a link between abortion and breast cancer were among those excluded. That is, of the 41 studies that have been published to date, 29 actually show increased risk of breast cancer among women who have chosen abortion. (Epidemiologists call this a "positive association.") Of these 29 studies, 17 are statistically significant; and of these 17 significantly positive studies in the literature, 10 were excluded from the Beral et al. analysis. In fact, if the results of the 15 studies excluded for unscientific reasons or not mentioned at all are averaged, they show an increase in breast cancer risk of 80 percent among women who have had abortions.

Beral et al. also separately compiled the studies into two types: those that used retrospective methods of data collection (i.e., interviews of breast cancer patients versus control subjects), and those that used prospective methods (i.e., medical records taken long before breast cancer diagnosis). The studies that used retrospective methods (39 studies) showed a significant overall 11 percent increase in risk with abortion. The studies that used prospective methodology (13 studies) showed a significant 7 percent decrease in risk with abortion. Instead of reporting the results of their findings accurately (that is, that the retrospective studies showed that abortion increases the risk of breast cancer), Beral et al. instead declared that these studies were simply unreliable because of "recall bias." Despite the theoretical possibility that recall bias exists, tests for such bias have proven negative, as was discussed above.

Finally, at least three of the studies based on prospective data merit exclusion from the Beral study because of vast gaps in their databases, and consequent misclassification of subjects.[22] The

Melbye study, discussed above, is one such study that should have been excluded.

Not an Independent Risk Factor

Many in the medical community will affirm that there is an increased risk of breast cancer among patients who choose abortion, but say it is simply because these women fail to receive the benefit of risk reduction by carrying the pregnancy to term. In other words, a woman who has had an abortion is comparable to a woman who chooses to start a family later in life. She is merely delaying a pregnancy and is no worse off having had an abortion than if she had never become pregnant at all.

Physiologically, the comparison is not at all apt; a woman who has an abortion *is at a greater risk* for breast cancer than the woman who simply delays having children. As explained above, this is because early on in pregnancy, Type 1 and 2 lobules, in which cancers are known to arise, proliferate in a woman's breasts; it is only after 32 weeks gestation that the pregnant woman's breasts mature into cancer-resistant Type 3 and 4 lobules. An abortion leaves the woman with an increased number of immature Type 1 and 2 lobules, thus more places for cancers to arise. So it is true that a woman who had an abortion loses the protective effect of a full-term pregnancy just as a woman who delayed childbearing does. However, the woman who had the abortion has also been left with a greater number of immature breast lobules as a result of once being pregnant. Because of this, the woman who had the abortion will be at a higher risk for breast cancer than a woman who has never been pregnant. Whether a woman's pregnancy is ended through induced abortion or by premature delivery, the physiology is the same: the woman has more places for cancers to arise. There is no medical dispute that premature deliveries cause increased breast cancer risk.

Organized Medicine Fails to Support Data

If abortion increases the risk of breast cancer, why does organized medicine fail to support and publicize the data? The intimidating political climate surrounding abortion is surely to blame. Doctors fear the repercussions to their name and their career if they disclose what is already known about the ABC link.

In my own case, I have worried that I would lose referrals from ob-gyns who perform abortions when I have lectured on this topic. Even a family doctor who had referred numerous patients said to me, "You don't tell my patients *that*, do you?" I worried about my practice. I can understand why a Harvard professor of risk assessment at a Boston cancer institute would tell me privately that she knew abortion was a risk factor for cancer but would not bring it up in her talks on risk (meanwhile encouraging *me* to speak out about it). She might lose her job. I have a colleague who did lose an appointment at a medical school in New York because he was quoted as giving credence to a study supporting the ABC link in the medical journal *Lancet*. One pro-choice epidemiologist who co-authored a study evincing a link between abortion and breast cancer told me she refused to speak on the topic anymore because she was tired of "having rocks thrown at her."

I learned what that felt like firsthand when I presented a research project in a session at the San Antonio Breast Cancer Symposium in December 2001. Although the abstract had been accepted six months earlier and had the word "abortion" in the title, the program director accused me of using his meeting as a platform to hand out anti-abortion literature. More troubling is that several years ago, the president of the American Society of Breast Surgeons told me that her board did not want to have a speaker on the subject at their meeting because they felt it was "too political." I argued that it was actually medical, not political, but to no avail. The director of the Miami Breast Cancer Conference also felt it was "too political." He returned a check I had given him to pay for an exhibit table at the conference.

Despite the silence about the ABC link on the part of those in the field of breast cancer, not one authority in the field to whom I have spoken directly has claimed that the data are not true or that I am wrong about the science.

Fear of malpractice litigation may be another reason for the silence. A case in Australia was settled in favor of a woman who had not been warned about the risk of breast cancer and the damage to her mental health before her abortion. The first medical malpractice case by a patient against an abortionist and clinic in the United States was settled on October 17, 2003. The patient had sued on the basis of lack of informed consent concerning the abortion–breast cancer link and the psychological sequelae.[23]

Doctors as a whole are well meaning and try to help their patients. It is very difficult to accept the fact that their well-intentioned practices may actually harm patients. Yet the medical community's disregard of lifesaving medical evidence is not without precedent. In 1840, forty years before Robert Koch developed the germ theory, a resident in obstetrics named Ignaz Semmelweis noted that there was a 25 percent mortality rate from childbed fever on the doctors' ward, while on the midwives' floor, where there was frequent hand washing, the mortality rate was only 2 percent. When at his suggestion an experiment was done by having doctors wash their hands, the infection and death rate on their ward was greatly reduced. Instead of rewarding Semmelweis and promoting hand washing to reduce mortality, the hospital directors fired and vilified him. It would take another forty years for the established medical community to accept the connection between frequent hand washing and reduced mortality.

Conclusion

In an editorial response to the furor raised by Dr. Joel Brind's landmark 1996 meta-analysis confirming that a preponderance of the data supported the ABC link, Dr. Stuart Donnan, editor-in-chief of the *Journal of Epidemiology and Community Health,* suggested the following to his "pro-choice" colleagues:

> I believe that if you take a view (as I do), which is often called "pro-choice," you need at the same time to have a view which might be called "pro-information" without excessive paternalistic censorship (or interpretation) of the data.[24]

The lives of thousands of women might be saved each year were other such physicians to follow Dr. Donnan's advice.[25]

NINE

The Psychological Aftermath of Three Decades of Abortion

E. JOANNE ANGELO, MD

IT IS WELL KNOWN THAT THE DEATH of a child is a particularly difficult loss to mourn. This is keenly understood in intensive care nurseries, where parents are encouraged to hold their baby after his or her death, to take pictures, to plan a funeral and a burial. Parents of aborted babies, however, have not been given permission to grieve. They have no memories, no pictures, no funeral service, and no grave to visit. As time passes and they become more aware of the reality of their truncated parenthood, their grief may become overwhelming. Waves of unexpected emotion—sorrow, emptiness, guilt, depression, suicidal thoughts—may flood them on the date the child would have been born, the anniversary of the abortion, Mother's Day, Father's Day, the birth of another baby, a death in the family. Mothers are often poignantly aware of a sense of emptiness and a longing for their children. The book of Jeremiah in the Bible speaks of Rachel weeping for her lost children: "Rachel mourns for her children; she refuses to be consoled because her children are no more."[1] In our society too, parents are weeping, silently and with shame, for their lost children. A tidal wave of sorrow and remorse is building in our time, but has not been recognized until recently.

Giving Sorrow Words, a book by Australian journalist Melinda Tankard Reist, gives voice to dozens of women, the stories of whose abortion experiences—and the years of turmoil and suffering that followed—had never been told.[2] The stories of these women were selected from those of 250 women, ranging in age from teens to seventy years old, who had responded to ads that Reist had placed in women's magazines and to newspaper accounts of the book she was planning to write chronicling post-abortion grief. Some of these 250 women sent Reist one page, others hundreds of pages.

Several of the accounts from *Giving Sorrow Words* are quoted below alongside stories of other contemporary women who have similarly experienced the tragedy of abortion in their lives. The following analysis also draws upon my twenty-eight years of clinical experience and research as a psychiatrist. In the confines of my office, many women have shared their experiences of pregnancy loss; it has become clear, over the years, that grief after abortion should be included among perinatal losses that must be mourned.

Grief after Miscarriage

Many pregnancies end in spontaneous miscarriage. Textbooks in obstetrics and gynecology estimate the number to be from 12 to 31 percent of all pregnancies; estimates are higher when very early miscarriages are taken into account. A recent article in the *American Journal of Maternal/Child Nursing* states,

> We know from studies of women ... that miscarriage is a life-changing event, and that women experience feelings of emptiness, dread, guilt and grief. They have an increased need for support and they have many fears about their future childbearing. ... Women have elevated depression and anxiety scores for up to a year after the event.[3]

Common themes for women after miscarriage are anger and frustration, guilt, feeling alone or that no one can really comprehend the depth of the sorrow, and feeling numb with grief. All of the women in the study published in the *American Journal of Maternal/Child Nursing* reported feelings of guilt about having caused the miscarriage, even though most of them stated they knew, in fact, that they probably had not.

Here are two accounts of the psychological pain women experienced after miscarriage:

> In the beginning I cried all the time. I couldn't go down the aisle at the supermarket. My soul was empty. My body was empty.

> The miscarriage was overwhelming. Overwhelming sadness and mourning. I was devastated. I sat in the house for two weeks. I wanted to be alone. I didn't want to talk to anyone. It was even hard for me to go to church.[4]

Many women suffer in silence after miscarriage, especially if the loss occurs in the course of infertility treatment. Fortunately, the grief women experience after miscarriage is finally being recognized, and supportive services are becoming available to them.

Grief after Abortion

After an induced abortion, many women suffer these same feelings with even greater intensity and over a much longer time—ten, twenty, thirty, forty years or even an entire lifetime. After all, unlike women who have miscarried, women who have had abortions feel guilty because what happened to them was due to choice.

Women agonize over their decision to have an abortion—a decision often made hurriedly, under duress, or in a clandestine manner. The father of the baby may insist on the abortion, or a teen mother's own parents may bring her to an abortion clinic. Confused by her ambivalent feelings about the pregnancy, and finding no one to help her find another solution, a woman experiencing a crisis pregnancy may believe that abortion is her only alternative, as the following accounts illustrate:

> My husband gave me an ultimatum: go and get an abortion or he would leave. As the sole parent's pension was an absolute pittance in those days, I felt that I had no choice. ... inside myself I was thinking, "Oh please don't let this happen; I want to keep this child; I think it will be a boy, a

lovely little brother for my daughter." (Zelda from Melbourne)[5]

As I had been brought up in a very religious family, I felt that I couldn't embarrass my family and so had no other choice but to have the abortions. (Ro, age 17)[6]

I felt betrayed by my body and angry that it had let me down. I felt hostile towards the child that had invaded my body. I felt I was being punished for enjoying a relatively casual sexual relationship. (In fact my feelings about him weren't casual ... but it soon became apparent that his feelings for me were.)

 I was repulsed by the thought of getting fat, developing stretch marks and of my breasts sagging. However, I also felt secretly proud that I could get pregnant and felt strangely protective towards the baby. Such contradictions. Even as I was plotting to kill it, I was also nurturing it. I stopped smoking and drinking, was careful about what I ate and what I lifted. (Catherine, age 28)[7]

In her book *The Anatomy of Bereavement,* Beverly Raphael discusses the complex process of grieving after induced abortion:

For many women there will be grief to follow and often an undue burden of guilt as well. It is particularly difficult for the woman that she seeks on the one hand to be rid of the pregnancy, yet at the same time mourn its loss.... The woman may have required a high level of denial of her tender feelings for the baby to allow her to make the decision for termination. This denial often carries her through the procedure and the hours afterward, so that she seems cheerful, accepting, but unwilling to talk at the time when supportive counseling may be offered at the clinic.[8]

Denial or repression of emotional responses may continue for weeks, months or years, especially in the woman's contacts with health care providers associated with her abortion experience. (This may seriously distort follow-up studies by abortion providers.) In the hours and days immediately following an abortion, pain and bleeding remind the woman of the physical assault on her body; endocrine changes cause her to become emotionally labile.

She is expected to conduct herself as if nothing significant has happened. Her efforts to comply with these social expectations may be at great personal expense. She may dose herself with alcohol and sleeping pills to deal with insomnia, nightmares, flashbacks to the abortion procedure, and the overwhelming sense of grief and guilt. She may throw herself into intense activity—work, study or recreation—or attempt to deal with her feelings of loneliness and emptiness by binge eating alternating with purging or anorexia. She may work intensely to repair destroyed intimate relationships or develop new ones inappropriately. All along she may berate herself for not "feeling fine," as she believes is expected of her.

Complaints of abdominal discomfort, painful sexual intercourse or infertility may lead her to seek treatment from one physician after another unsuccessfully. The very examinations and invasive procedures to which she is subjected may cause flashbacks to the abortion procedure, causing great difficulty and anxiety for her and for her physicians.

The following are quotations from more of the Australian women as they put words to their sorrow:

> I am tormented. . . . I've lost self-esteem, inner peace, find it very difficult to find joy anywhere in life, am always depressed. I'm taking Luvox [an antidepressant] and use alcohol . . . and marijuana to cope with the pain of living. I always feel sad and ashamed. . . . He or she would have started school next week. (Julie)[9]

> I often wonder what happened with my baby. Where did they put her. . . . was she buried or just thrown away like some piece of rubbish? Sometimes I think of just ringing the clinic and ask them what they did with all the babies, but then, what am I expecting they'll tell me!! . . . all through the day I wonder how she would look, and how it would have been having her around with my two sons. . . . Whenever I'm asked how many children I have, I refrain from saying three! Nadia is always on our minds. (Carrie)[10]

I had such a deep sense of betraying the baby who clung within me, it trusted me and I was its only love.... After I gave birth to my first child, the reality of pregnancy kicked in. Now I could see the end result and I felt very sad for my lost baby. (Renaee, who had an abortion at age 17)[11]

I had paid the ultimate price. I have to live with myself. I have to look at myself and know it was my choice—I did it. I can't believe I did it, I wish I could change everything and go back.... I will never be forgiven for what I did. (Mother of four who gave no name or address)[12]

My boyfriend told me if I kept it, it would break us apart. I loved him and I went and destroyed a life which I wanted so much. I was eighteen weeks pregnant, it took me three days for the operation. Men don't understand what you go through and I wish they did. Throughout the three days I had needles all the time and nausea. This was because of love. I always think of other people before my own feelings, but look at where it's gotten me.... I felt empty, like I had no soul in me.... My boyfriend said to me a couple of days afterwards that we might end up being married and we could have a family together. I said I couldn't marry someone that made me destroy a baby. (Lisa, age 19)[13]

Although typically an abortion is undergone to preserve a relationship, few women can bear to spend their lives with the men with and for whom they have committed this act.

Late-Term Abortions

Even abortion advocates agree that psychiatric complications may follow late-term abortions like Lisa's. The mother has had more time to experience the reality of her pregnancy. She has often felt the baby move and seen him or her on the screen during an ultrasound examination. She may even have a picture of the baby.

Late-term abortions are often done because of suspected fetal abnormalities or retardation. Parents and siblings are left to wonder how close to perfect one must be to deserve to live. Imagine the impact on a five-year-old of being told, "The baby was not okay so the doctor sent him back to God."

Late-term abortions take a longer time. The cervix is softened over several days by the use of medications that make the woman feel miserable. If the procedure is a partial-birth abortion, the baby is partially delivered, killed in the birth canal, and the skull is crushed. Memories can haunt women for life.

On the day that President Clinton vetoed the bill that would have banned partial-birth abortions, five women who had gone through this grisly procedure spoke at a press conference—presumably to endorse his decision. Yet they referred to their experience as a "personal and family tragedy," a "nightmare," "the loss in my heart." One woman's story is particularly poignant:

> ... my husband and I are Jewish and we got the news [that their unborn child had been diagnosed with a congenital anomaly] on Rosh Hashanah. And we finally had the procedure. The third day of the procedure, it was Yom Kippur, the holiest day of the Jewish year. And Yom Kippur is the day that you mourn those that have passed, and it's the day that you pray that God will inscribe them in the book of life. We'll forever mourn our son.[14]

Many babies with severe birth defects will not live until their expected date of delivery. There will be a need to grieve their deaths. However, after aborting them, their parents are further burdened by the guilt of having caused their deaths to occur prematurely and violently. Alternative obstetrical methods recommended by obstetricians would allow the child to be delivered alive and intact. In the case of intrauterine death, vaginal delivery can be induced quickly. The opportunity to see and hold even a defective baby after delivery or death is a help to the grieving process.[15] The congenital anomalies that are incompatible with life are seldom revealed in the monstrous physical appearance that parents often have fantasized.

An Ocean of Grief

The stories of women who have suffered the tragedy of abortion should be considered a sample of the waters from the ocean of grief and suffering caused by three decades of abortion on demand. The tide in this ocean is rising. Women who have previously been silent are being encouraged to speak out about their firsthand experience with the tragedy of abortion, and they are doing so in large numbers. The women in Melinda Tankard Reist's book, for instance, were grateful for the opportunity to share their sorrow—even with a complete stranger whom they would probably never meet.

> So many feelings and emotions, locked in the secret hall-ways of my heart and mind! But it helps knowing that I am not the only one going through all this.... Thank you for taking the time to listen to women like me, who so far felt all alone in a world that cannot understand the pain, frustration and guilt one goes through after an abortion. (Cassie)

> Write your book, and please tell the truth, about the pain, the shattered lives. Abortion is an open, bleeding wound. (Anita)

> Writing my story has been the best (and only) therapy I have had since I fell pregnant seventeen years ago.... I have wanted to cry this out to the world for years. (Linda)[16]

After a trusting relationship has formed, in the privacy of a psychotherapist's office, women may dare to tell their experiences of abortion and its aftermath—feelings of remorse, guilt and shame, depression, substance abuse, failed relationships, eating disorders, post-traumatic stress disorder, suicidal thoughts. Yet sometimes even experienced therapists and distinguished psychiatrists do not understand. Women are often told that abortion is common, that it could not explain their symptoms. These symptoms are then treated without any exploration of their root cause. Sleeping pills, antidepressants, anti-anxiety medication and substance-abuse programs are prescribed. Women are thus convinced that there must be something terribly wrong with them because they have not been able to "just get over it" and "get on with their lives" as other women seem to be able to do.

When permission is finally granted to speak about their abortion experiences in a compassionate environment, the floodgates open. Years of dammed-up emotions are released. This can be overwhelming to the listener. It cannot be contained in a fifty-minute session or in the confessional ten minutes before Mass.

Post-abortion grief does not just affect mothers of aborted children. Each of these babies has a father as well. Dr. Vincent Rue writes about "forgotten fathers" who must also grieve their lost children.[17] Some must deal with the guilt of having insisted that their children be aborted, having paid for the abortion, or having done nothing to try to stop it. Others must deal with the fact that they were unable to protect their unborn children, since fathers have no legal rights regarding the decision to abort.[18]

Grandmothers of aborted children also grieve. Some of them must face their own role in bringing their daughter to an abortionist. For some, their daughter's abortion reopens the unhealed wound of their own decision to terminate a pregnancy years before. And then there are the roommates, friends and siblings of the women who chose abortion, and the sisters and brothers of the aborted children. In various ways, their lives are also affected. Guidance counselors and school nurses who recommend and arrange abortions for students also must deal with their role in the death of these babies. The nurses and physicians who perform abortions are often profoundly affected in their own lives.

Published Epidemiological Studies

The psychiatric literature is finally beginning to publish evidence of the enormity of the problem—not only in individual case studies, which have always been a highly valued method of understanding the human psyche, but also in epidemiological studies using objective statistical data from public records.

In 1996 the *British Medical Journal,* for instance, published a study documenting the rates of suicide after pregnancy in Finland.

Using data from national heath registers in which all births and
deaths are recorded, researchers studied the rates of suicide during
the year after the end of a pregnancy. The rate of suicide for women
who had experienced live birth (5.9 per 100,000) was about half
the rate for all women of childbearing age (11.3 per 100,000). The
suicide rate associated with abortion (34.7 per 100,000) was nearly
six times greater than the suicide rate after live birth. These statistics appear to indicate that childbirth protects women from suicide. Abortion, on the other hand, seems to increase the risk of
suicide sixfold compared with successful pregnancies.[19]

The *American Journal of Orthopsychiatry* in July 2002 published
an article comparing first-time use of outpatient mental health
services during the four years after an abortion or a live birth. Data
were collected from a state-funded medical insurance program in
California known as Medi-Cal. Obstetrical and mental health
claims for the same patients were reviewed. The rate of mental
health claims was 17 percent higher for the abortion group in
comparison with the birth group.[20]

Using the same data pool from Medi-Cal, an article in the
Southern Medical Journal in August 2002 found significantly higher
rates of death among women after abortion than among women
who had given birth. These data included death from suicide, acci-
dents, AIDS, circulatory disease and cerebrovascular disease. The
authors concluded that the higher death rates associated with
abortion may be explained by self-destructive tendencies, depression, and other unhealthy behavior aggravated by the abortion
experience.[21]

Helping Women Resolve Their Grief

There is hope for women who have lost children through abortion. I know many women who have worked through their mourning, healed the wounds—physical, psychological and spiritual
wounds caused by their abortions and the tumultuous time afterward—and gone on to be happy, productive citizens, parents and
friends. Many of these women have helped others to make better
choices in their lives or to heal similar wounds.

Women under my psychiatric care who have had abortions have often been referred because of serious and even life-threatening symptoms such as depression, post-traumatic stress disorder, or other anxiety disorders. In addition to offering them appropriate medications and the safety of psychiatric hospitalization if necessary, I work with them in psychotherapy.

Our first task is to revisit their abortion experience in all its sordid details as well as the circumstances that led up to it. This may be the first time they have shared with a nonjudgmental listener the anguish of their ambivalent feelings and the pressures that catapulted them into their "choice." The particular experience of the abortion procedure may have been so horrific for a woman that she has locked it away in the recesses of her mind, only to have it appear in recurrent nightmares and flashbacks at unpredictable times. There is often great relief from being able to express the fright, pain, anger and remorse. To verify the reality of long-suppressed memories, we will at times request records from the abortion clinic or hospital.

Next, a woman must accept her own role in the decision to have an abortion and face the terrible burden of guilt and shame that she has buried for years. For some women, the loss they must mourn in the early stages of working through the trauma of abortion is the loss of their sense of self. "How could I have done something like this? I always thought I was a good person. I would never hurt anyone." Although at one level a woman is well aware that the child she was carrying died, she may not yet be ready to do the work of mourning her dead baby.

The difficult circumstances around the pregnancy and the abortion decision are explored in detail in the early stages of psychotherapy. The woman usually comes to understand that her decision was not made with the requisite freedom from fear, time for consultation and deliberation, consideration of viable alternatives or support in choosing anything but the abortion.

Women often believe they have committed an "unforgivable sin." They may have stayed away from church or sacraments for years; or they may have attended a healing service or mentioned their abortion among a list of other things in confession, but then say, "I still feel terrible, so I know it didn't work." They are expecting spiritual healing and sacramental reconciliation to subdue psychological pain that may last for years. For them, something besides psychotherapy is indicated.

Helping to Heal the Wounds of Abortion: Project Rachel

The Catholic Church has always offered pastoral counseling and the Sacrament of Reconciliation (also called confession or penance) to women in these circumstances. In 1984 a new program was launched in the Archdiocese of Milwaukee to reach out actively to women and men seeking to resolve an abortion loss. "Project Rachel" is now present in 144 dioceses in the United States and in several other English-speaking countries. When a person calls a designated telephone number, while remaining anonymous, she (or he) is referred to a priest or psychotherapeutic professional who offers to help heal the wounds of abortion.

In addition to individual visits with a counselor and/or priest, assistance is offered to women in psychotherapy groups, support groups or opportunities to meet one-on-one with other women who have had similar experiences and have resolved their grief. There are annual memorial masses for babies who died before birth through miscarriage or abortion, memorial gardens to visit, and special rooms or chapels where a woman can go to pray in silence and find a Book of Remembrance in which to inscribe the name she has given to the child she has lost through abortion.

In Project Rachel and in psychotherapy a woman finds a place to share the personal representations of her lost child she has formed in her mind. At first her image of the baby may be a nightmare of violent dismemberment, sometimes based on what she has seen at the abortion clinic. Over time she is able to visualize her baby at peace, "living in the Lord," as Pope John Paul II describes in the passage below.[22] As the years go by, women often mark each successive birthday the child would have had and remember him or her silently at holidays and family gatherings.

The Project Rachel brochure for the Archdiocese of Boston contains a moving outreach message to women who have had abortions from Pope John Paul II's encyclical, *Evangelium Vitae (The Gospel of Life):*

> I would now like to say a special word to women who have had an abortion. The [Catholic] Church is aware of the many factors which may have influenced your decision, and she does not doubt that in many cases it was a painful and even shattering decision. The wound in your heart may not yet have healed. Certainly what happened was and remains terribly wrong. But do not give in to discouragement and do not lose hope. Try rather to understand what happened and face it honestly. If you have not already done so, give your-selves over with humility and trust to repentance. The Father of mercies is ready to give you his forgiveness and his peace in the Sacrament of Reconciliation. You will come to understand that nothing is definitively lost and you will also be able to ask forgiveness from your child, who is now living in the Lord. With the friendly and expert help and advice of other people, and as a result of your own painful experience, you can be among the most eloquent defenders of everyone's right to life. Through your commitment to life, whether by accepting the birth of other children or by welcoming and caring for those most in need of someone to be close to them, you will become promoters of a new way of looking at human life.[23]

Conclusion

Three decades of abortion on demand have created an ocean of sorrow and grief in the hearts of women, often concealed at great personal expense. This rising tide of grief is just beginning to be discovered by others as these women find a voice to tell what a tragedy abortion has been in their lives.

Their sorrow will not be in vain. As "eloquent defenders of everyone's right to life," quietly and almost imperceptibly, they will create new ripples of hope and peace based on an understanding of God's infinite love and mercy and the truth about the dignity of human persons at all stages of development. These women will offer us the opportunity to learn to love unconditionally and to empathize with their sorrow and that of everyone whom their abortion has touched. In the words of Pope John Paul II, "suffering is present in the world in order to release love, in order to give birth to works of love toward neighbor, in order to transform the whole of human civilization into a civilization of love."[24]

PART III
Abortion, Law, Regulation and Alternatives

TEN

The Supreme Court and the Creation of the Two-Dimensional Woman

PAIGE COMSTOCK CUNNINGHAM, ESQ.

ONE GENERATION AGO, SEVEN MEN wrote a document that radically altered the lives of American women and American culture.[1] In *Roe v. Wade* (and its companion case, *Doe v. Bolton*), the Supreme Court not only legalized abortion on demand; it did so based on a jarring view of women and their participation in society. Its distorted picture portrayed women as isolated individuals, and society as not responsible to them or to their children.

At the time of the decision in *Roe*, abortion had been held out as the solution to social problems such as domestic violence, overpopulation, poverty, child abuse and illegitimacy, as well as the panacea for the psychological and emotional distress of unplanned pregnancy. Rather than expect society, in its constituent parts, to seek constructive remedies for these troubling problems, the Court placed the onus squarely on the shoulders of women—and the decision was hailed as a giant step forward in women's equality.

The Supreme Court reaffirmed the legal right to abortion nearly twenty years after *Roe* in *Planned Parenthood v. Casey*, a decision that also upheld a variety of state regulations on abortion while denying the right of the spouse to be notified of the abortion. Like *Roe*, the judgment in *Casey* rested on similarly ill-conceived notions of women's needs and the legal underpinnings of women's equality. *Casey*, contrary to the Court's claims, did not satisfactorily settle the abortion issue. Instead, it further delayed progress toward a culture that encourages the recognition of women as relational beings.

More than a generation after *Roe* and more than a decade after *Casey,* it is time to mend this torn picture of women and the ties that bind them to others. Women are embedded in relationships, capable of courage, sacrifice and coping with the challenge of an untimely pregnancy—so long as they are given the support they need.

The legal doctrine of abortion on demand, created by *Roe* (and *Doe*), *Casey* and subsequent cases, is an anomaly in American jurisprudence, public policy and culture. It is time to assess its real impact on women and women's equality.

Roe v. Wade: "Women's Liberation" Cloaked in Medical Paternalism

Roe v. Wade is one of the most celebrated, reviled, reviewed, criticized and analyzed Supreme Court opinions ever rendered. There is no point in repeating those analyses here, but it is worth considering the two-dimensionality of the Court's view of women and women's capacities.

Roe's lack of a jurisprudential foundation has been thoroughly discussed. Justice White, a dissenter to the opinion, called it "an exercise in raw judicial power."[2] In writing for the Court, Justice Blackmun himself acknowledged that the "Constitution does not explicitly mention any right of privacy";[3] instead, he maintained that the ephemeral foundation for the "zones of privacy" might be embedded in the First Amendment, the Fourth and Fifth Amendments, the "penumbras" of the Bill of Rights, the Ninth Amendment, or "in the concept of liberty guaranteed by the first section of the Fourteenth Amendment."[4] Despite his hesitation to claim any particular constitutional authority, Blackmun was quite adamant that the right of privacy "is broad enough to encompass a woman's decision whether or not to terminate her pregnancy."[5]

The Court, however, ultimately intended the abortion decision to be exercised by the woman's doctor. In his summary, Justice Blackmun reiterated: "(a) For the stage prior to approximately the end of the first trimester, the abortion decision and its effectuation must be left to *the medical judgment of the pregnant woman's attending physician.*"[6] Until viability, "the abortion decision in *all* its aspects is inherently, and primarily, a *medical decision, and basic responsibility for it must rest with the physician.*"[7] According to *Roe,* the physician is also the one who determines if his patient should have an abortion *after* viability, by evaluating medical, emotional and social factors.

In its nearly single-minded focus on the medical aspects of the abortion decision, the Court ignored the unique relationship of mother and unborn child. Justice Blackmun merely concluded that the "potential human life" of the fetus is secondary to the mother's, since "the unborn have never been recognized in the law as persons in the whole sense."[8] Thus, the state's interest in the fetus ("potentiality of human life") was thought to be separate and distinct from its interest in the health of the pregnant woman. Mother and child were thus cast in an adversarial posture, with the mother's interest always triumphant.

The Court did not attempt to reconcile the interests of mother and of child or see them as interrelated. According to *Roe,* the mother has an unqualified right to an abortion during the first trimester, and the decision is left to her doctor. After the first trimester, a state could regulate abortion in order to protect maternal health, that is, to make abortion safer for the mother. After viability, which the Court said is the time when the child could live outside the womb (even with artificial aid), the state could "even proscribe abortion." In its now-famous limitation to state regulation of abortion, however, the Court stated that abortion must be permitted after viability when "necessary for the preservation of the life or health of the mother."[9] Thus, even when the fetus merits some state protection, since it "presumably has the capability of meaningful life outside the mother's womb,"[10] this "meaningful life" is rendered meaningless if the mother claims any health reason for her abortion.

And just what does "health" entail? "Maternal health" was explained in *Roe's* companion case, *Doe v. Bolton,* which the Court directed to be read in conjunction with *Roe.* Again, the woman's physician was the one to decide whether an abortion was justified. "[His] medical judgment may be exercised in the light of all factors—physical, emotional, psychological, familial, and the woman's age—relevant to the well-being of the patient. All these factors relate to health."[11] Needless to say, this is a virtually limitless interpretation of maternal health.

Justice Blackmun gave specific examples in *Roe:* "[M]aternity, or additional offspring ... a distressful life and future ... psychological harm ... child care ... the unwanted child ... the problem of bringing a child into a family already unable, psychologically and otherwise, to care for it [*sic*] ... [the] continuing stigma of unwed motherhood ..."[12] Thus, the physician is entrusted with making not only a medical judgment about the effect of continued pregnancy on the woman's body, but also nonmedical judgments regarding factors such as the emotional impact of the pregnancy, the number of children she has, and whether she has a husband or an intact marriage. Note that none of these "detriments," as the Court called them, has to do with the pregnancy itself. Instead, as Notre Dame law professor Gerard Bradley notes, "these 'detriments' were about *raising children.* .... [T]hese reasons justify infanticide as much as they do abortion."[13]

By including a variety of social factors as medical justifications for abortion, the abortion doctrine releases others from their responsibility to help women ameliorate those conditions. The burden thus falls on women to abort children who might make things worse.[14] Women are simply offered abortion, the quick fix, while genuinely meaningful solutions to their social or personal problems are left unexplored.

Some pro-choice feminists acknowledge this reality. Caroline Whitbeck, for instance, calls abortion a "grim option," one that is "selected only because of a still greater aversion to the only available alternatives."[15] Those grimmer alternatives include permanent disability caused by pregnancy, being reduced to poverty, subjecting oneself or one's children to abuse, and the stigma of illegitimacy. The availability of abortion, according to Whitbeck, has curtailed the development of adequate care for women and children, safe and effective contraceptives, and efforts to make women more financially stable. She writes:

> The literature on abortion shows that many people are readily able to image themselves in the place of the fetus but not

in the place of the pregnant woman, but if one is able to look at the matter from the perspective of the pregnant woman, it becomes clear how much violence is done to the woman by abortion, and therefore that the woman's self interest would lead her to avoid (unwanted pregnancy and) abortion if she had other options genuinely available.[16]

Legalized abortion has delayed the development of creative alternatives to abortion that affirm a woman's desire to give birth. The availability of abortion alleviates pressures on families, employers, schools, churches and the government to build a culture that welcomes new lives. As long as abortion is legally a woman's constitutional right, she sees the burdens of childbearing and parenthood as hers alone; its joys escape her consideration.

Evolution of the *Roe* Doctrine: Abortion on Demand

Although Chief Justice Burger made a point of stating in his *Doe* concurrence that "the Court today rejects any claim that the Constitution requires abortions on demand,"[17] that was precisely the effect of *Roe* and *Doe* as they were interpreted in subsequent cases. In the first few years, the Court struck down virtually every regulation of abortion: a ban on abortion advertising,[18] spousal consent,[19] parental consent,[20] prohibition on saline amniocentesis (a "salting out" procedure that a fetus occasionally survived),[21] requirements that the abortionist use professional skill and care to preserve the fetus's life,[22] and employ the technique most likely to cause the live birth of a viable unborn child.[23] The Court rejected a law mandating use of the abortion method most likely to preserve the fetus's life, and requiring that a second physician be present at post-viability abortions (for the purpose of treating the child, if he or she survived).[24] No regulation in behalf of the unborn child passed constitutional muster in those early years. Even a requirement that fetal remains be disposed of in "a humane and sanitary manner" was odious to the Court.[25]

Regulations to promote maternal health did not fare much better. Although the Court professed concern for the mother's health and her ability to make a fully informed choice, its rulings proved otherwise. The Court struck down a Pennsylvania law that required physicians to inform their patients of fetal development, the medical risks of abortion, and public health reporting mandates.[26] It struck down a waiting period (giving the woman time to make her decision without pressure from abortion clinic employees).[27] Making one minor concession to maternal health, the Court upheld a state law mandating a pathology report to ensure that the abortion was complete.[28]

The Court was somewhat more solicitous of teenagers. It eventually approved parental consent legislation, but with the condition that states include a judicial bypass (in reality, a parental bypass) procedure for the minor to prove that she is mature enough to make her own decision, or that the abortion would be in her best interests.[29]

Abortion advocates' attempt to push for abortion funding seemed to be the only public policy transformation at which they failed. They claimed that taxpayers should fund abortions for poor women, challenging the federal Hyde Amendment (which excluded abortion from Medicaid coverage except where the mother's life was endangered) as well as state Medicaid laws. The Court upheld the Hyde Amendment[30] and the states' rights to decline taxpayer funding of abortion procedures.[31]

In the years leading up to *Planned Parenthood v. Casey* in 1992, however, the Court's hard-line opposition to protective regulations relaxed somewhat. This was not due to any newfound insight, but to newly appointed justices. In a 1989 decision, the Court narrowly approved Missouri's requirement of testing for fetal viability at 20 weeks gestation, and a ban on the use of public facilities or public employees in the performance of abortion.[32] A ban on the use of Title X funds for counseling or referring for abortion was also upheld.[33]

Protection for "Chosen" Children

Despite the expansion of the abortion doctrine in the years following *Roe*, legislatures continued to maintain and develop greater legal protection of the unborn child in all contexts except abortion. Prior to *Roe,* it was already settled law that the unborn child could inherit property, have a guardian *ad litem* appointed to represent his interests, be the subject of a custody dispute, and be considered a child for purposes of terminating the parent-child relationship.

Thirty-one states and the federal government now have fetal homicide laws, which punish third parties (people other than the mother or the abortionist) who kill an unborn child. Some fetal protection laws were on the books before *Roe,* but many states subsequently expanded their reach: many of these laws now apply from conception onward, rather than only after quickening or viability. In one case, a man was convicted of fetal assault even though the mother was unaware that she was pregnant.[34] In many states, someone who batters a pregnant woman and injures the fetus may be charged with two crimes: against the mother and against her unborn child. The child may also recover in a civil action for injuries suffered in the womb. The Unborn Victims of Violence Act of 2004 (known as "Laci and Conner's Law") applies this principle to anyone who injures or kills an unborn child during the commission of a federal crime.[35]

It is counterintuitive that legislation should be necessary to protect an infant who survives an abortion. But prosecutors argued that they had no statutory basis for prosecuting abortionists, nurses or hospitals that abandoned tiny abortion survivors to gasp out their last breath in a utility closet, without medical attention. The Born-Alive Infants Protection Act, passed in 2002, protects these children.[36] The law stipulates that any child born alive after an attempted abortion must be treated like any other person and given necessary medical care. This nondiscrimination law ensures that all newly born children will be treated equally, regardless of how their mothers intended to end their pregnancies.

Prenatal care has been extended to the unborn children of poor mothers who otherwise would not qualify for assistance. When New York extended its Prenatal Care Assistance Program to women up to 85 percent above the poverty line, Planned Parenthood and abortion clinics sued to stop the program; they were outraged that New York did not offer abortion as part of "prenatal care." Fortunately, they were unsuccessful.[37]

Recently, the Department of Health and Human Services clarified its policy to include unborn children in S-CHIP (State Children's Health Insurance Program). Thus, prenatal care may be provided for fetuses whose mothers otherwise would not qualify for aid.[38] Rather than welcome this measure as a way to help women have healthy pregnancies and healthy children, abortion advocates attacked it as "a ploy to create new grounds for outlawing abortion,"[39] a "guerilla attack on abortion rights," and "another way to undermine the rights of women."[40] For advocates of abortion, the right to abort children seems to be threatened by the opportunity to care for them.

The federal government also protects the fetus from nontherapeutic medical research. Any research must be for the benefit of the fetus, or pose no more than minimal risk to the fetus, and have the purpose of gaining knowledge that cannot be obtained through any other means.[41] This protection was established in 1974, after abortion was legalized.[42] Clearly, the government understood its responsibility to protect the fetus outside the abortion context.

Planned Parenthood v. Casey: Abortion and Women's Equality

In the years immediately prior to *Planned Parenthood v. Casey* (1992), abortion advocates and opponents alike predicted the possibility of a Supreme Court reversal of *Roe v. Wade.* Advocates vehemently argued that *Roe's* reversal would "turn the clock back on women's rights," claiming that abortion rights were essential to eliminating sex discrimination against women. Without abortion on demand, they contended, women would continue to be oppressed and treated unequally.

But in fact, *Roe v. Wade* is not essential for any constitutional right, save the right to abortion itself. Women's increased access to economic and legal equality has come by way of thousands of laws passed at the national, state and local levels, and by court rulings—as well as through the determination and hard work of individual women. Indeed, none of the very substantial legal progress that has opened new possibilities for women over the last thirty years rests on *Roe.*[43]

Rather than promote women's equality, abortion has, in fact, hurt women. Only women experience any immediate or long-term physical complications, emotional devastation or psychological trauma that may result from abortion, as poignantly described elsewhere in this volume. Legalized abortion has shifted primary (and often sole) responsibility for the bearing and rearing of children onto women's shoulders. Abortion has cheapened relationships between women and men, and has shredded the moral fabric of American culture.[44] The Court had an opportunity to put a stop to this deterioration when it heard oral arguments in a challenge to the Pennsylvania Abortion Control Act in April of 1992.

• • •

THE COMMONWEALTH OF PENNSYLVANIA had passed commonsense abortion regulations: informed consent with a 24-hour reflection period, one-parent consent (with the requisite judicial waiver), spousal notice, a medical emergency exemption, and a record-keeping/reporting requirement. In the highly fractured decision of *Planned Parenthood v. Casey*, the Supreme Court upheld all provisions of the law except spousal notice. After *Casey*, then, states could at least moderately regulate abortion to protect maternal health.

Many abortion advocates reacted to the decision in *Casey* as if the Court had slammed the door on women's rights—as if abortion on demand were in jeopardy. In fact, however, the *Casey* Court reaffirmed *Roe v. Wade* and the abortion doctrine.

In an unusual joint opinion (three justices—O'Connor, Kennedy and Souter—writing together, rather than one writing and others signing), the Court once again tried to resolve the national controversy over abortion.[45] Once again, it failed. The opinion is at times incoherent, and overall it is breathtakingly arrogant. As Justice Scalia wrote in his scathing dissent, "The Imperial Judiciary lives."[46]

Planned Parenthood v. Casey bears little resemblance to *Roe v. Wade*. In restating what it called the "essential holding" of *Roe*, the joint opinion revised virtually every aspect of *Roe*.[47] While *Roe* had divided pregnancy into trimesters, the joint opinion in *Casey* divided it into pre- and post-viability phases. Where *Roe* described abortion as a privacy right, *Casey* found it to be a "liberty." Rather than cite history reaching back millennia, in *Casey* the justices followed their own "reasoned judgment." Unlike *Roe*, the *Casey* opinion did not characterize abortion as a fundamental right (like other rights protected by the Bill of Rights), nor did it give clear guidance on what standard of review courts should employ to determine whether state abortion regulations are constitutional.[48]

Also missing from *Casey* is the distinctly medical tone of *Roe*. Where *Roe* said that abortion in all its aspects is a medical decision, *Casey* essentially removed the physician from the decision-making equation. Likewise, *Casey* did not directly address the social factors and stressful circumstances that were so important in *Roe*. Perhaps this is because these woes have not been ameliorated with the advent of legalized abortion.[49]

But even though the Court in *Casey* abandoned virtually all of its prior reasoning in *Roe,* it still found a basis for reaffirming the abortion right: society "needs" it. In its decision, the Court examined whether there were any reasons *not* to uphold *Roe*. For our purposes, the most significant of these inquiries was whether *Roe* could be reversed "without serious inequity to those who have relied upon it or significant damage to the stability of the society governed by it."[50] The justices maintained that although individual women could change their sexual behavior "virtually imme-diate[ly]" if abortion were not available to deal with the consequences of spontaneous sex or birth control failure, it was unlikely that society as a whole could react to the sudden absence of abortion. This "general reliance" on abortion by society at large most influenced the Court's decision. The reasoning in *Casey* thus rested less on the case of a woman needing abortion in the midst of tragic circumstances than on the representation of a society accustomed to abortion's easy availability.

The observations in the joint opinion reveal a distressingly narrow view of women and men. Justices O'Connor, Kennedy and Souter simply could not imagine American culture without abortion: "For two decades of economic and social developments, people have organized intimate relationships and made choices that define their views of themselves and their places in society, in reliance on the availability of abortion in the event that contraception should fail."[51] A presumed societal reliance on abortion was transformed into a legal justification for affirming it as a constitutional right.

Women's equality, in the justices' view, could not be achieved outside of our abortion-dependent culture. "An entire generation has come of age free to assume *Roe's* concept of liberty in defining the capacity of women to act in society, and to make reproductive decisions. . . ."[52] It is a peculiar view of women to see their efficacy and equality as social actors as being based solely on their legal access to abortion.

Perhaps what underlies this arrogant and elitist presumption is the view of abortion as less of a fail-safe for a woman in a true crisis pregnancy than a form of contraception to be used by the ambitious career woman. That is, rather than understand abortion as the solution to the problem of unwanted children, the stigma of illegitimacy or psychological stress, as *Roe* did, *Casey* was far more concerned with women's ability to get ahead and feel good about themselves. The Court's pregnant woman was transformed from Jane Roe, a poor, single mother with several children, to Murphy Brown, the confident, independent woman who chooses her destiny according to "her own conception of her spiritual imperatives and her place in society."[53]

For the *Casey* Court, then, abortion was foundational to women's power to maintain their "places in society": "The ability of women to participate equally in the economic and social life of the Nation has been facilitated by their ability to control their reproductive lives."[54] Yet, as Chief Justice Rehnquist pointed out in his dissent, it is incorrect and even condescending to presume that women have achieved their "places in society" as a result of the right to abort:

> The joint opinion's assertion of this fact is undeveloped and totally conclusory. In fact, one cannot be sure to what economic and social development the opinion is referring. . . . Surely it is dubious to suggest that women have reached their "places in society" in reliance upon *Roe*, rather than as a result of their determination to obtain higher education and compete with men in the job

market, and of society's increasing recognition of their ability to fill positions that were previously thought to be reserved only for men.[55]

Justice Rehnquist and the other dissenting justices understood that women are most truly equal when their success—whether in politics, employment, economics, education or influence—is seen as based on their own competence, rather than on their legal capacity to terminate pregnancies by abortion.

Women's First Right?

Do women see legal access to abortion as their most cherished right? Surveys say no: "Polling data consistently demonstrate that abortion is not even close to being the most important issue in women's lives."[56] Polls reveal various sets of priorities, depending on women's age, family status, and whether it is election season. During the 2000 campaigns, top issues were education and taxes, according to the Polling Company.[57] "Among women with children, polls consistently show that balancing work and family is at the top of the list of concerns."[58]

Abortion may seem omnipresent and always anxious to expand its domain, but it is not comfortably established in our national life. Indeed, opposition to abortion is growing, especially among younger people. They tend to be more opposed to abortion than the baby-boomer generation.[59] And more of them are willing to ban it completely: "Nationwide, one-third of people ages 18 to 29 said abortion should never be legal. That contrasts with about 23 percent for those ages 30 to 64, and about 20 percent for those over age 65."[60] Other research confirms this trend. Fred Barnes, a nationally known political commentator and executive editor of the *Weekly Standard,* recently noted that "[f]ocus groups have found [young people] to be surprisingly tilted against abortion. A poll of college freshmen in 1996 found that only half backed efforts to keep abortion legal, down from 65 percent in 1990."[61]

Although occasionally people do move from a pro-life to a pro-choice position, they do so in far lower numbers than the other direction. According to a recent Zogby poll, "22 percent said they were less in favor of abortion today than they were a decade ago. About half that number said they were more in favor of it."[62] Public opinion is arrayed not just against the morality of abortion, but also its legality. According to a recent Wirthlin Worldwide poll, nearly 70 percent of all Americans prefer "restoring legal protection to unborn children." And 66 percent want justices appointed to the Supreme Court "who would uphold laws that restore legal protection to unborn children."[63] A Zogby poll revealed that only 22 percent think abortion should always be permitted.[64]

More and more, the ranks of pro-life women include career women, feminists and even left-wingers.[65] And they are increasingly drawn from the younger generation. An August 2003 Gallup Youth Survey revealed that "most U.S. teens (aged 13 to 17) do not consider abortion to be morally acceptable."[66] Women are not just changing their opinions about abortion; they are also changing their behavior. The number of abortions has declined from 1.6 million to 1.3 million a year. The abortion rate peaked in 1981, with 29.3 women per 1,000 women ages 15 to 44 undergoing the procedure. The rate declined to 21.3 per 1,000 in 2000. The largest drop has been among teenagers.[67]

• • •

MANY HAVE COME TO ADMIT THAT the sexual revolution, featuring abortion on demand, has simply not benefited women. Patricia Dalton, a clinical psychologist in Washington, D.C., sees many women in her practice whose lives are in chaos. They are involved in a series of casual relationships—"hookups"—with men who enjoy the sex, but reject the permanent commitment of marriage.

> The sexual revolution of four decades ago was meant to liberate women. Instead, it has left too many of them flailing around with a faulty blueprint for life. . . . Take the two basic realities that shape women's sexual lives in very different ways from men's. First, a woman's child-bearing years are finite, while men have the luxury of time. Second, there is the social convention, found all over the world, that men seek mates the same age or younger, while

women mate with men close to their age or older. Young women ignore these realities at their peril. Those women who have embraced both word and deed of the sexual revolution can find that the years of fertility pass pretty quickly. [68]

Moreover, easy access to abortion puts additional pressure on women to deny their fertility during the years in which they are most likely to have healthy pregnancies and healthy children. Instead, women have sacrificed those few years of fertility to men's sexual desires. The easy availability and legality of abortion removed the one remaining reason a woman had to say "no" to sex. After all, she and her (potential) partner both know that if her contraception fails, she can still get an abortion.

In the eyes of men who have enjoyed women's increased sexual availability, who have sloughed off old wives and acquired young "trophies" under the sanction of no-fault divorce, *who encouraged abortions*—thus avoiding responsibility for children they have bred—and who will send women into combat, women are not uniquely precious individuals but merely easily disposable sex objects.[69]

Only women can become pregnant and bear children. To insist that women have the capacity to become "un-pregnant" at will is to demand that women become more like men.

Instead of handing women the abortion option as a condition for maintaining their "places in society," why not engage in the more demanding task of enabling women to welcome the children they conceive? Because women experience both the discomforts and the astonishments of pregnancy, it would make sense to ask women what would make pregnancy and childbirth more bearable. Women know what they need to avoid the "grim" option of abortion.

In the research that she did in preparation for founding the Nurturing Network, Mary Cunningham Agee interviewed women who had had abortions. The factors that would have enabled them to continue their pregnancies included options that made sense in terms of their education and professional life: quickly and discreetly transferring to a new college or another job; finding a supportive place to live during the final months of the pregnancy; continuing their education without losing credits or financial aid; and practical resources to enable them to continue their life plans and to include a child in their revised future.[70]

Frederica Mathewes-Green likewise conducted in-depth listening sessions with women who had abortions they later regretted. When she asked what would have made the biggest difference in their decision, to her surprise many of the women responded: a friend. The current relationships of the women had had the greatest impact on their decision. They often had the abortions to please boyfriends (usually out of the picture soon afterward) or husbands, or to protect their parents. As a woman named Cheryl said, "[I]f I had one person rallying on my side, I could have made it. . . . [I]f I had had one person say, 'Cheryl, don't [have an abortion]. Do like you did with the other baby. Leave this jerk. Go ahead and give it up for adoption.' I would have done it in a minute."[71]

The Isolation of Abortion: A Caricature of the Three-Dimensional Woman

The Supreme Court in *Casey* subtly acknowledged, but then aided and abetted, the radically individualized nature of abortion. The Court admitted that abortion is "fraught with consequences for others," those who perform and assist in abortion, the spouse, family and society, and "depending on one's beliefs, for the life or potential life that is aborted."[72] Yet those consequences, no matter how profound, may not override the woman's "intimate," "deep" and "personal" definition of "[her] own concept of existence, of meaning, of the universe, and of the mystery of human life."[73] Her "concept of meaning and existence" may lead her to choose abortion when she sees no other viable option for continuing her life plans—or her motive might be as shallow as wanting to fit into a bridesmaid's dress, or as discriminatory as preferring a boy to a girl.

The Supreme Court helped to perpetuate such isolation for the aborting woman in denying the importance of her relationship with her husband, the unborn baby's father. The Pennsylvania statute at issue in *Casey* had provided that he was entitled to notice (not consent) of the proposed abortion, unless his wife certified that he was not the father, he could not be located, he sexually abused her, or she feared physical harm if he found out about the pregnancy. But despite the stipulation that the spouse was excluded from notice in those circumstances where he was most likely to be irresponsible or abusive, the Court still found the spousal notice provision unconstitutional. It decided that as between the two individuals within a marriage, only one of the partners could prevail in a disagreement over abortion. In this regard, the male was wholly separate and unequal.

Even though Pennsylvania carefully excluded abusive husbands from its spousal notice provision, the Supreme Court excluded *all* husbands: "A husband has no enforceable right to require a wife to advise him before she exercises her personal choices."[74] Astonishingly, the Court weighed the husband's interest in his unborn child as no more significant than his interest in contraception, his wife's smoking or drinking during pregnancy, or "any type of surgery that may have complications affecting the husband's interest in his wife's reproductive organs."[75] This prohibition on spousal notice applies throughout the pregnancy. Under such a view, the state has a stronger constitutional interest in the viable fetus than even the fetus's own father does.

The relationship with the woman's husband is thus given short shrift by the courts, on a par with boyfriends, who have no rights.[76] Yet both groups of fathers have an unrelieved responsibility to pay child support if their partner decides to proceed with the pregnancy. A husband or a boyfriend may have to pay even if he is *not* the baby's father.[77]

Parents of minor teenagers may have the opportunity to be notified of their daughter's proposed abortion under this decision, but the emphasis is on "may." With the friendly help of an abortion clinic salesperson, she can get a judge to rubberstamp her abortion decision, efficiently bypassing her parents.[78]

A woman or a teenage girl often aborts to spare her parents shame or to preserve a relationship. The sacrifice often fails. "Studies of abortion and its aftermath reveal that, more often than not, relationships do not survive an abortion: the majority of unmarried couples break up either before or soon after an abortion."[79] Married couples may not fare much better. Sue Nathanson wrote about the abortion of her fourth child, a decision she made in response to pressure by her husband ("I am absolutely clear that I do not want a fourth child under any circumstances"). The night before her abortion, she sat by her window and "grieved and grieved and grieved and grieved."[80]

The Changing Nature of Parenthood

Perhaps one of the most devastating, and possibly unintended, consequences of legalized abortion is a change in the nature of parenthood. Recent advances in prenatal testing permit parents to screen their unborn child, both *in utero* and *in vitro,* for a variety of genetic conditions. Ultrasound, amniocentesis and chorionic villi sampling are offered to pregnant women. None of these is 100 percent accurate, and healthy children may be incorrectly diagnosed as unhealthy. Hundreds of genetic conditions may be detected, but virtually none can be treated in the womb. Writer Elizabeth Kristol reveals the pressure on women to abort if a fetal defect is indicated: "Within the medical literature there is a clear assumption that counselors are there, in effect, to help patients through the difficult process of *agreeing* to be tested and *agreeing* to abort in the event of a diagnosed defect."[81] Lori Andrews, an international genetic and reproductive technology adviser, warns of the impact of these tests: "the mere existence of a [genetic] technology contains an implicit coercion to use it. . . . Sometimes the coercion is more than implicit."[82]

Just whom does all this testing and aborting benefit? Certainly not the mother. Abortion on account of genetic defects is more traumatic than the parents anticipate, and "almost always more traumatic than abortion in the event of an unwanted pregnancy," writes Kristol.[83] Andrews agrees, saying that "The lives of some of these families might have been disturbed less by the birth of an affected child than by the termination of pregnancy."[84] Prenatal testing pressures parents to ensure that their child meets certain standards before they commit to giving birth. These dilemmas about what genetic risks are acceptable have led to what Barbara Rothman calls "the tentative pregnancy,"[85] delaying the bonding between mother and unborn child. Andrews writes that "parents are increasingly feeling that they are put into the position of playing God."[86]

Genetic testing benefits the companies, patent holders and physicians who produce and administer the tests. It benefits public health agencies that proudly cite reductions in the number of disabled people, quietly ignoring the fact that this is attributable almost exclusively to abortion and not to any medical advances. It benefits physicians who fear professional liability if a child they deliver is born with disabilities. It benefits taxpayers, who will not have to fund medical care for these children. Genetic testing also benefits insurers, who encourage its use in order to exclude coverage if parents choose to bear a "defective" child.[87] A National Institutes of Health task force on prenatal diagnosis stated: "There is something profoundly troubling about allowing the birth of an infant who is known in advance to suffer from serious disease or defect."[88] But does this testing benefit society itself?

Legalized abortion and the abortion mentality encourage discrimination against those who do not meet the approval of geneticists, doctors, insurers, parents or society. Again, in Elizabeth Kristol's words: "Through the gradual introduction of new forms of technology and testing, the medical establishment and the public health sector have been developing subtle quality-of-life standards and not-so-subtle ways of discouraging the birth of those who do not measure up."[89] If abortion were not such a convenient option, it is likely that more funding would be directed into treating and curing these conditions. As long as abortion is the "cheap" alternative, it will be foisted on women who actually want their children, women who might find to their surprise that they are quite capable of rising to the challenge of raising a child with disabilities.

Legalized abortion also gives encouragement to oppressive employers. Even though pregnancy discrimination in employment is prohibited by Title VII of the Civil Rights Act of 1964, some employers still use unfair tactics to keep pregnant employees from continuing their pregnancy.

When Sharrona Alexander was assistant women's basketball coach at the University of California at Berkeley, she was told that she couldn't handle the job if she continued her pregnancy, and that she should either have an abortion or quit. Ironically, the head coach who issued the ultimatum was Marianne Stanley, who had given birth when she herself was a college basketball player.[90]

Female EMT trainees in Washington, D.C., were similarly warned by their supervisor that they would be terminated if they got pregnant during their first year of employment.[91] There again, the "guilty" supervisor in this case was a woman. In the same vein, the New York City Department of Corrections settled a lawsuit filed by several female officers who were told to have abortions. Many who refused were given physically grueling jobs.[92]

Women in professional careers are not exempt from such pressure. One study of female medical residents reported open hostility to pregnant residents from program directors and colleagues.[93] Those physicians and residents who chose childbirth were "more likely to underreport their symptoms in order to minimize the influence of their pregnancy on their work."[94] Their abortion rate was three times higher than in the control group. The *National Law Journal* reported on the problem of workplace environments that are not supportive of working mothers.[95] Women who want to make partner in their law firm are discreetly advised not to get pregnant until partnership is secure; otherwise, they may be put on the "mommy track."

We Can Do Better

As long as abortion on demand remains legal and a constitutional right, women will continue to be isolated and exploited. Women do not need abortion for full equality. We do not need abortion for economic, political or legal rights. We do not need abortion to protect our families, ourselves, our futures. We do not want abortion as the first resort to preserve relationships that are precious to us. Abortion hurts women. Abortion hurts husbands and grandparents. Abortion hurts all of us.

It is time to stop.

ELEVEN

Abortion Clinic Regulation

Combating the True "Back Alley"

DENISE M. BURKE, ESQ.

IN THE LATE 1960s AND EARLY 1970s, abortion proponents assured judges, legislators and the public that legalizing abortion would be beneficial to the health and well-being of American women. In support of these arguments, they devised a litany of purported "advantages" of legalized abortion, including increased medical safety.

First, proponents argued that if abortion was legal, it would be safer for women because it would become an accepted part of "mainstream medical care," proper surgical practices would be followed, and skilled and reputable gynecologists and surgeons would perform the procedure. Unskilled and incompetent "butchers" would no longer perform abortions.

Second, legalized abortion would eliminate the five to ten thousand deaths that abortion advocates disingenuously claimed resulted from illegal or so-called "back-alley" abortions each year.*

---

*The numbers of deaths from illegal abortion were greatly exaggerated, however, as were the claims that abortions were inherently unsafe before *Roe v. Wade*. For example, in 1960, Planned Parenthood's director Mary Calderone wrote:

> Abortion is no longer a dangerous procedure. This applies not just to therapeutic abortions as performed in hospitals but also so-called illegal abortions as done by physicians. . . . [A]bortion, whether therapeutic or illegal, is in the main no longer dangerous, because it is being done well by physicians."

Who can forget the image they chose to represent the tragedy of an illegal abortion: the coat hanger—a jagged, unsanitary and certainly unsafe surgical instrument.

Finally, legalizing abortion would ensure that women received proper care before, during and after the procedure. Proper care would obviously include appropriate postoperative monitoring and follow-up care. Legalized abortion would ensure that no woman would bleed to death—alone and in pain following an unsafe abortion.

These were the promises. But has it proven to be the reality? Has more than thirty years of legal abortion eliminated these problems? Or have abortion clinics across the nation become the true "back alleys" of abortion mythology?

Unsafe and Substandard Conditions

A quick review of just a few cases of substandard abortion care poignantly contrasts the reality of abortion in America today with what abortion advocates promised that legalizing abortion would accomplish. Clearly it has not eliminated substandard medical care; nor kept people without medical licenses from performing abortions; nor ended the use of unsanitary procedure rooms and unsterilized, inadequate instrumentation; nor ensured competent post-abortion care; nor prevented women from dying due to unsafe abortions.

Mary Calderone, "Illegal Abortion as a Public Health Problem," *American Journal of Public Health* 50 (July 1960): 949.

Moreover, Dr. Bernard Nathanson, a founder of National Abortion and Reproductive Rights Action League, later conceded that these statistics were intentionally misleading:

How many deaths were we talking about when abortion was illegal? In NARAL, we generally emphasized the drama of the individual case, not the mass statistics, but when we spoke of the latter it was always "5,000 to 10,000 deaths a year." I confess that I knew the figures were totally false, and I suppose the others did too if they stopped to think of it. . . . The overriding concern was to get the laws eliminated, and anything within reason which had to be done was permissible.

Bernard Nathanson, *Aborting America* (New York: Doubleday, 1979), 193.

- In 1994, several women testified before the General Assembly of the South Carolina legislature that when they walked into some of the state's abortion clinics, they saw bloody, unwashed sheets, bloody cots in recovery rooms, and dirty bathrooms. Clinic workers testified that the remains of unborn children were not disposed of properly, but rather rinsed down sinks.[1]
- An undercover news team entered a Baton Rouge, Louisiana, abortion clinic and videotaped rusty surgical instruments and blood-spattered surgical tables and floors.[2]
- Witnesses in Texas disclosed that abortion clinic personnel without medical licenses or formal medical training perform abortions.[3]
- In Arizona, a young mother bled to death from a two-inch laceration in her uterus. As she lay in what medical assistants described as a "pool" of blood that soaked the bedding and ran down her legs, the woman was heard crying for help and asking what was wrong with her. Where was her doctor? He was eating lunch in the break room, refusing requests to check her condition; he later left her bleeding and unconscious to visit his tailor. The woman died after bleeding for two or three hours, although a hospital emergency room was less than five minutes down the street.[4]

Tragically, these events are indicative of what some American women experience when they enter an abortion clinic. The question is what can be done about it. Each of the states involved in these appalling incidents and practices has since enacted comprehensive regulations requiring abortion clinics to be licensed by the state, to be inspected by state health department officials, and to meet minimum health and safety regulations. But there should be a national effort to eliminate substandard medical practice at the nation's abortion clinics.

Why Should States Regulate Abortion Clinics?

Enacting comprehensive regulations is a critical and sensible solution to the problem of unsafe abortions in the "back-alley" abortion clinics of America. These regulations are designed to safeguard against unsanitary conditions, inferior equipment, and the employment of unsuitable and untrained personnel. They are also intended to put an end to substandard medical practice that injures and kills women each year.

More importantly, the abortion industry often refuses to police itself, focusing instead on profit margins rather than investing in women's health and safety. While state legislators debate and enact regulations to protect the women of their states from substandard and unsafe conditions and practices at some abortion clinics, lawyers for the abortion industry prepare and file legal challenges seeking to invalidate the regulations.

Clearly, states have the authority to intervene and the duty and responsibility to act when a public health problem exists. One woman's death is too many. One woman left infertile because of infection caused by unsanitary conditions is too many. One woman rushed bleeding to an emergency room with a punctured uterus, because her abortion provider was in a hurry to complete as many abortions as possible in one afternoon, is too many.

Each year, women are injured during abortions or suffer complications from the procedure. In attempting to determine just how many women are injured by abortion each year, we can begin with the abortion industry's own very "modest estimates." A 1995 review of information collected by the National Abortion Federation (NAF) revealed that .08 percent of women suffered complications requiring hospitalization, .05 percent reported an infection, .12 percent reported continued pregnancy following an attempted abortion, and .03 percent suffered uterine perforation.[5] Moreover, according to data collected by the U.S. Centers for Disease Control and Prevention (CDC), approximately one woman in 100,000 dies from complications associated with a first-trimester abortion.[6] The mortality rates for later-term abortions are significantly higher and the risk increases with advancing gestational age. For example, at 11 to 12 weeks gestation, the morality risk is 1 in 100,000, but at 16 to 20 weeks gestation the risk is 7 in 100,000.[7]

At first glance, these statistics may not seem significant. However, there were 1.31 million abortions in the United States in 2000 (a slight decrease from the 1.36 million reported in 1996).[8]

With the abortion industry's own statistics as a basis, it is clear that thousands of women are being injured by abortion each year and that some of them die.

We do not know the numbers of women injured or killed during legal abortions. For the last thirty years, the CDC and the states have, with greatly varying degrees of success, attempted to share and collect information on abortion; but states are not required to submit abortion data to the CDC.[9]

Currently, forty-six states require that some abortion-related data be reported to their own health departments. The types of information collected differ, but generally include raw data on the kinds of facilities performing abortions, demographic character-istics of women undergoing abortions, and information about the procedure itself including the type of abortion performed.[10] Con-spicuously absent from many state reporting statutes is a require-ment to report abortion-related complications. As the author of a leading abortion textbook writes, "[T]here are few surgical proce-dures given so little attention and so underrated in its potential hazard as abortion."[11]

This lack of comprehensive and dependable information on abortion complications points to a need for a system of national abortion reporting standards. Such standards would provide more accurate and reliable information as to how many women suffer from physical and psychological problems related to abortion and how many die from abortion-related complications.

What Is the Current Status of State Regulation?

At present, twenty-three states enforce some degree of regulation on abortions whether they are first-trimester or later. The scope and effectiveness of these regulations vary widely, however. States like Arizona, Louisiana, Mississippi, South Carolina and Texas have comprehensive and detailed regulations. Other states such as Florida, Georgia and Massachusetts impose only minimal admin-istrative requirements.[12]

A few states simply require that certain later-term abortions be done in hospitals or surgical centers, thus subjecting only those particular abortions to the more stringent health and safety requirements that apply to those types of facilities.[13] Meanwhile, six states, including Minnesota, New Jersey and Virginia, only impose minimum health and safety standards on abortions done after the first trimester.[14]

Obviously, there is a great need for states to review their existing regulation of the clinics, as well as physicians' offices and other facilities that perform abortions. In the past, there was some reluctance to do this in the face of threats of costly and time-consuming litigation by abortion providers and advocacy groups. But in light of recent court victories affirming the constitutionality of state abortion clinic regulations, the effectiveness of this threat has significantly diminished.

Where Do the Regulations and Standards Originate?

Normally, state health department employees and committees formulate abortion clinic regulations. State health departments typically regulate many other types of medical practices and draw on that experience in crafting suitable regulations for abortion clinics. They often reference and utilize inspection protocols and regulatory standards formulated for other types of medical practices, including other invasive surgical procedures. These standards impose minimum requirements for sanitation, sterilization, necessary emergency equipment, and postsurgical monitoring of patients for bleeding, pain and other complications.

The law recognizes, however, that "abortion is a unique act."[15] The U.S. Supreme Court in *Planned Parenthood v. Casey* stated that:

> the abortion decision ... is more than a philosophic exercise. Abortion is a unique act. It is an act fraught with consequences for others; for the woman who must live with the implications of her decision; for the spouse, family, and society which must confront the knowledge that these procedures exist, procedures some deem nothing short of an act of violence against innocent human life; and, depending on one's beliefs, for the life or potential life that is aborted.[16]

Moreover, courts have also recognized that for the purposes of regulation, abortion is distinct from other routine medical services because of the "particular gravitas of the moral, psychological, and familial aspects of [the] abortion decision."[17] Therefore, state health departments must necessarily devise specific standards tailored to meet the needs of women undergoing abortions.

Where do state health departments get information and input on appropriate abortion-specific protocols? Significantly and somewhat surprisingly, this information comes from the abortion industry itself.

The National Abortion Federation (NAF) and Planned Parenthood, among other pro-abortion advocacy groups and organizations, have formulated and published standards and guidelines for affiliated clinics and physicians. In fact, Planned Parenthood clinics, with few exceptions, must adhere to the operational standards and protocols mandated by the Planned Parenthood Federation of America. State legislatures have obtained copies of these standards and protocols and have used them to formulate minimum health and safety standards for abortion care.

What Do Abortion Clinic Regulations Typically Cover?

Abortion clinic regulations require that clinics and physicians' offices performing a specified number of abortions be licensed and inspected by state officials. Moreover, a comprehensive set of clinic regulations will typically delineate standards for administration and staffing, prescribing minimum personnel qualifications and requirements for written policies and procedures.

Current state clinic regulations also stipulate minimum requirements for equipment, sanitation, and proper maintenance of patients' medical records. These normally include such "controversial" requirements as having stethoscopes, blood-pressure cuffs and sufficient sets of surgical instruments in procedure rooms, and maintaining a "smoke- and vermin-free environment."

To ensure that patients receive competent and safe abortions, the regulations also typically require clinic staff to obtain detailed medical histories, perform important laboratory tests, make accurate estimates of gestational age, and provide patients with written instructions for postoperative care and handling complications. Further, each clinic is typically required to have on site during operating hours at least one physician who has admitting privileges at a local hospital.[18]

None of this is controversial; it is simply good medicine. Any clinic that cares about providing quality patient care would meet and, in all likelihood, exceed the standards prescribed by these regulations.

What Arguments Are Made Against Clinic Regulations?

Despite the fact that states are utilizing standards and protocols drafted and championed by the abortion industry, abortion providers and advocacy groups are repeatedly challenging these regulations in federal court.[19] In the late 1970s and early 1980s, abortion proponents were able, using the federal courts, to invalidate attempts by states to regulate the provision of abortions. For twenty years after *Roe v. Wade*, regulatory standards were routinely struck down as unconstitutional.[20]

In 1992, however, the U.S. Supreme Court in *Planned Parenthood v. Casey* determined that courts had gone too far in striking state regulations and restrictions on abortion. The Court confirmed that regulations designed to ensure maternal health, which did not "unduly burden" a woman's right to choose abortion, were constitutionally acceptable.[21] So, the battle began over how much regulation, what could be regulated, and to what extent.

In the late 1990s, a few states began enacting comprehensive and detailed abortion clinic regulations in response to tragic deaths and strikingly substandard conditions at some clinics. Abortion proponents, rather than cooperate with state officials to ensure women's health and safety, launched a new series of legal challenges. Ignoring the obvious health benefits of these standards, their widespread acceptance within the medical community, and the fact that they were modeled on standards promulgated by abortion advocacy organizations, abortion providers and attorneys for the industry have repeatedly challenged the constitutionality of these regulations.

First, abortion proponents argue that the regulations impose a constitutionally impermissible burden on women seeking abortions. Basically, the argument is that these regulations will raise the price of abortions and women will not be able to afford them. But attorneys for the industry, despite multiple opportunities, have not produced a shred of credible evidence to support this contention. Instead, a careful review of their purported evidence clearly shows that it is the abortion providers who will have to spend more money to meet these standards, and it is their "bottom line" that might be harmed.[22] Common sense dictates that women are protected, not burdened, by these regulations.

Abortion providers also argue that the regulations unfairly single out abortion for "special treatment" and that other "similar" procedures are not being regulated. They argue that this violates their rights to equal treatment under the law.[23] It is instructive, however, to look at what procedures they claim are "similar": removal of moles, cervical biopsies, and ear, nose and throat surgery. Clearly, none of these is comparable to abortion, a procedure that the U.S. Supreme Court and most Americans have recognized is a unique act with unique consequences and risks.

Further, abortion proponents routinely argue that the regulations are vague. Without hesitation, doctors with years of schooling and clinical experience contend that they don't know what "smoke-free" means, what "sufficient sets of surgical instruments to meet patient needs" means, or even what "gestational age" or "first trimester" means.

Finally, in a desperate attempt to strike down regulations with which they do not want to comply, abortion proponents have unsuccessfully argued that a requirement that patients' medical records be reviewed as part of an inspection protocol violates privacy rights. They further assert that inspections of clinics to ensure compliance with regulatory requirements violate the Fourth Amendment,[24] and that mandates for clergy to be made available to women who request their counsel violate the principle of "separation of church and state."[25]

What Is the Current Status of Litigation?

The U.S. Supreme Court has not specifically ruled on the constitutionality of state abortion clinic regulations. In recent years, several states, including South Carolina, Texas and Arizona, have had
to defend their respective regulations against legal challenges by
abortionists and advocacy groups.[26]

In February 2001, the Supreme Court refused to hear an
appeal of rulings in the South Carolina case.[27] The U.S. Court of
Appeals for the Fourth Circuit had found that the state's regulations were constitutional, did not violate equal-protection guar-
antees, and did not create an "undue burden" on women seeking
abortions.[28] With typical persistence, however, abortion proponents challenged the South Carolina regulations on additional
grounds in late 2001. The challenges were rejected and the regulations were subsequently upheld, in September 2002.[29] In upholding them for a second time, the appeals court determined that the
regulations did not violate patients' informational privacy rights,
did not violate the "separation of church and state," and were not
unconstitutionally vague.[30] In April 2003, the U.S. Supreme Court
denied review for the second time.[31]

In January 2003, Texas finally prevailed in the five-year legal
battle over the constitutionality of its abortion clinic regulations.
The U.S. Court of Appeals for the Fifth Circuit had ruled in 2001
that the Texas regulations did not violate equal-protection guar-
antees and did not "single out" abortion clinics for unfair over-
sight or treatment.[32] After the case was returned to the district
court in Houston, abortion providers filed a new complaint alleg-
ing that women seeking abortions were being denied their right
to equal protection under the law and that the regulations were
a form of improper sex discrimination. In April 2002, the district
court summarily rejected these new challenges and, in December
2002, dismissed the case.[33]

In December 2003, the U.S. Court of Appeals for the Ninth
Circuit in San Francisco heard the appeal of a lower court's deci-
sion substantially upholding Arizona's abortion clinic regulations.[34]
The district court in Tucson, consistent with the rulings in the

South Carolina and Texas cases, had determined in October 2001 that Arizona's regulations were a constitutional exercise of the state's authority to protect the health of women seeking abortions and were enacted in direct response to "specific incidents, including the death of Lou Anne Herron from complications associated with an abortion, where maternal health was impacted by substandard medical care."[35]

To date, each of these challenges has resulted in decisions substantially upholding the constitutionality of abortion clinic regulations. But all of these decisions have come from lower federal courts. In the next few years, we could see the U.S. Supreme Court deciding under what circumstances and to what extent states may regulate abortion clinics and provide for the health and safety of women.

TWELVE

Abortion-Alternative Legislation and the Law of the Gift

DORINDA C. BORDLEE, ESQ.

LISA BEAMER GAVE BIRTH TO HER third child, a baby girl named Morgan, on January 9, 2002. With the determined battle cry of "Let's roll," Morgan's late father, Todd Beamer, is believed to have helped overcome terrorist hijackers before United Airlines Flight 93 crashed near Pittsburgh on September 11, 2001. Morgan Beamer is only one of scores of children born after their fathers were killed on September 11.[1] Each reminds us of the enduring legacy of parenting, and of the unique and unrepeatable gift that is every human life.

And each of their mothers reminds us that Todd Beamer and his companions on Flight 93 were not the only ones to display heroic self-giving. There was also the quiet heroism of the women who courageously chose to bear the children of their lost loved ones despite intensely difficult circumstances. The courage of these women becomes even more noteworthy when set against the crassness of the September 11 response of Planned Parenthood of New York City: a limited-time offer of *free abortions* to Lisa Beamer and every other woman carrying the living reminders of their loved ones lost in the World Trade Center attacks.[2]

These women who chose life are witnesses to the meaning of genuine love, of that gift of self and of that acceptance of others which ought to be at the heart of every interpersonal relationship.[3] The many human dramas of September 11 seem to have stirred the national conscience to a growing renewal of respect for the dignity of the human person, which is magnified in heroic self-giving. This "law of the gift"—that men and women find human fulfillment in self-giving, not self-assertion—is foundational to abortion-alternative policies.[4]

Such policies are gaining ground despite the U.S. Supreme Court's abortion cases, which exalt the isolated woman by enshrining the principle of radical autonomy—an ideology positing that a woman can find fulfillment only by imitating male models of domination and self-assertion, even against her own unborn child.[5]

Such an ideology does not speak to the vast majority of women, who have or want to have families in addition to using their gifts and talents in the professional world. In an effort to reintegrate woman in solidarity with the whole human family in a more balanced way, it is time to question the Court's misconception of woman, and to nurture the beginnings of a new, more compassionate feminism that embraces the law of the gift.

The following two legislative initiatives are expressions of the law of the gift in that each reflects a policy that enables citizens to reach out with concrete resources and hands-on help to women who have the courage to choose life.

Government Funding of Pregnancy Support Centers

"Our business is to fight the poison of hopelessness with love." These words were spoken by Governor Robert Casey to Pennsylvania abortion-alternative service providers at the Second Annual Project WIN Conference in April 1997. Project WIN, an acronym for Project Women in Need, was instituted by Governor Casey in 1996 and has become a model by which Pennsylvania has led the way in government funding of abortion-alternative services.

Real Alternatives is the nonprofit organization that serves as the prime contractor in the administration of Project WIN. During the 2002–03 fiscal year, the program will reimburse over $5.3 million in combined state and federal funds to over 110 participating organizations in Pennsylvania that offer a wide range of alternative-to-abortion services. These include providing information, counseling, and support services that assist women to choose childbirth and to make informed decisions regarding the choice of adoption or parenting. The services are provided free of charge to women experiencing an unplanned pregnancy; women who reasonably believe they may be pregnant; and parents or legal guardians of an infant under twelve months of age.

Organizations that receive reimbursement from the program include pregnancy support centers (crisis pregnancy centers), social service agencies, adoption agencies and maternity homes. Specific examples of reimbursed services include pregnancy self-test kits, education on fetal development and nutritional needs, information on the risks of STDs, prenatal and postnatal education, education/GED referrals and vocational training, child care referrals, adoption service information, medical and insurance referrals, and parenting classes for the first twelve months after birth.

Project WIN also includes reimbursement for statewide marketing and media outreach so that women in unexpected pregnancies can be made aware that there are options other than abortion. This aspect of the program includes a statewide toll-free telephone referral system, television commercials, newspaper, bus and phonebook ads, and mailings to schools and hospitals.

Project WIN centers are nonprofit organizations staffed by caring professionals and trained counselors. Since the beginning of the program in March 1996, Project WIN centers have served more than seventy thousand women throughout Pennsylvania, and the program boasts steady drops in abortion choice percentages.[6] The reimbursed service providers do more than help lower the incidence of abortion. They simultaneously address many of the social, personal, familial and economic problems that often form barriers to self-sufficiency, marriage, parental involvement and healthy lifestyles.

In response to a letter from Congressman Joseph R. Pitts of Pennsylvania citing these aspects of Project WIN (January 15, 2002), the U.S. Department of Health and Human Services concluded that abortion-alternative services fit within the broad purposes of the Temporary Assistance for Needy Families (TANF) program.[7] The written reply from the Office of the Assistant Secretary, Administration for Children and Families (January 31, 2002) clarified the HHS policy that a state can indeed use TANF funds to reimburse pregnancy support centers, maternity homes and social service agencies that provide alternatives-to-abortion services.

Following this model and with assistance from Real Alternatives, Louisiana became the second state in the nation to appropriate TANF funding to abortion-alternative services, with a budget appropriation of $1.5 million for the 2002–03 fiscal year.[8]

Abortion-alternative funding is a public policy that reflects the law of the gift because it challenges the body politic—those of faith and those of no particular faith[9]—to reach out in solidarity to women and their unborn children with hands-on, woman-to-woman social services.

"Women's Right to Know" Laws: Informed Consent for Abortion

For too long, abortion providers have maintained power over women by controlling information about the nature of abortion, its medical risks, the baby's development, and the availability of alternatives-to-abortion resources. Outside of the abortion context, informed consent requirements are common and uncontroversial. Abortion is the only invasive medical procedure in which the generally accepted requirements for informed consent are disregarded and opposed by abortion rights groups.[10]

Clinics often provide inadequate and inaccurate information to women considering abortion. Anne Catherine Speckhard, Ph.D., of the University of Minnesota, in an article published in the 1992 issue of *Journal of Social Issues,* reported that 81 percent of the women she surveyed said they had felt victimized by the abortion process. These women felt either that they were coerced into the abortion or that important information about the pregnancy resolution and abortion procedure had been withheld.* In response to requests from many women who were physically and psycho-

---

*Regarding the feeling of being coerced into the abortion, it is interesting to note the results of "listening groups" of post-abortive women in six major cities reported in a book by Frederica Mathewes-Green, *Real Choices: Listening to Women; Looking for Alternatives to Abortion* (Conciliar Press, 1997). Overwhelmingly it was problems with *relationships,* not with practical matters of housing or finances, that were cited as the primary motive for the abortion decision. Appendix D of that book shows the following reasons:

logically harmed by abortion and were interested in helping other women to understand all the risks and consequences of abortion and the alternatives, states began to pass "Women's Right to Know" legislation.

Women's Right to Know laws specify two tiers of information to be provided to a woman at least twenty-four hours before abortion is to take place. On the first tier, either the referring or the attending physician will be required to give the woman the name of the doctor who is to perform the abortion, a description of the procedure to be used, the medical risks of the procedure as well as of childbirth, and objective information about the traits of the developing unborn child. The second tier requires that either the referring or the attending physician, or another qualified individual, give the woman a booklet containing color photographs of the developing unborn child at two-week intervals; information on medical benefits, the father's liability and adoption; and a directory of public and private agencies that can help the woman bring her child to term.

In 1992, the U.S. Supreme Court upheld the Pennsylvania Women's Right to Know law in *Planned Parenthood v. Casey*,[11] and refused to review a lower court ruling that found Mississippi's law to be constitutional.[12] The Court in *Casey* said, "In attempting to ensure that a woman apprehend the full consequences of her decision, the State furthers the legitimate purpose of reducing the risk that a woman may elect an abortion, only to discover later, with devastating psychological consequences, that her decision was not fully informed."[13]

The *Casey* Court upheld a 24-hour reflection period, specifically overruling a previous decision.[14] The Court said, "The idea that important decisions will be more informed and deliberate if they follow some period of reflection does not strike us as unreasonable, particularly where the statute directs that impor-

1. Husband/boyfriend pressured her to have an abortion	38.2%
2. Parents pressured her (in 6 of 7 cases, her mother)	20.5%
3. Woman wanted to protect parents	11.7%
4. Husband/boyfriend weak and unsupportive	8.8%
5. Woman afraid of parental disapproval	8.8%
6. Other	11.7%

tant information become part of the background of the decision."[15]

Twenty-three states now have Women's Right to Know laws,[16] taking advantage of *Casey's* language clarifying that "a State [may] further its legitimate goal of protecting the life of the unborn by enacting legislation aimed at ensuring a decision that is mature and informed, even when in so doing the State expresses a preference for childbirth over abortion."[17]

Right-to-know legislation reflects the law of the gift because it ensures that women are given the information they both need and deserve to enable them to make fully informed decisions. Scientifically accurate information that shows the beauty of unborn human life, as well as the significant medical dangers of abortion, will undoubtedly give more women the courage to offer to their unborn children that sincere and loving gift that is themselves.

Conclusion

Legislative policies that reflect the law of the gift are on the rise as a result of the hard lessons that the social experiment in legalized abortion has taught us over the past three decades. These initiatives spring up as women of all ages increasingly understand that our goal must be to balance and integrate family and professional life in a way that is both humane and distinctly feminine.

By her ability to experience a special union with the mystery of life as it develops in her womb, as Pope John Paul II says, woman "first learns and then teaches others that human relations are authentic if they are open to accepting the other person: a person who is recognized and loved because of the dignity which comes from being a person and not from other considerations, such as usefulness, strength, intelligence, beauty or health."[18]

The special gifts and talents that women offer in the context of both family and professional life position us to have enormous impact in rehumanizing our culture.[19] It is both the right and the duty of the body politic to propose a renewed vision of woman, one that will inspire life-affirming legislative initiatives to foster a more humane culture.[20]

About the Contributors

E. Joanne Angelo is a psychiatrist in private practice in Boston and an assistant clinical professor of psychiatry at Tufts University School of Medicine. Dr. Angelo has lectured nationally and written extensively on the negative effects of abortion on women, their partners and families. Most recently, Dr. Angelo contributed a chapter on post-abortion grief to a college textbook in abnormal psychology, published by Dushkin/McGraw-Hill.

Erika Bachiochi received her Juris Doctor degree from Boston University School of Law in 2001. Ms. Bachiochi was a Bradley Fellow at the Institute for the Study of Religion and Politics at Boston College, where she received her master of theology in 1999. She has lectured on women's issues and researched and written in the areas of welfare reform, education reform and marriage law. Ms. Bachiochi is the mother of two young children.

Dorinda C. Bordlee is an attorney who specializes in constitutional law in the field of bioethics, and is the mother of four young children. She has served as special assistant attorney general for the Louisiana Department of Justice, has lectured on abortion-related topics at all educational levels, and has frequently served as a pro-life media spokesperson. Ms. Bordlee is currently with the legal department of Americans United for Life.

Denise Burke is a staff attorney with Americans United for Life, specializing in constitutional law and bioethics. She also serves as a reserve judge advocate with the United States Air Force. She has extensive litigation experience, having served as a military prosecutor, a military defense attorney, a state prosecutor and a special assistant U.S. attorney. Ms. Burke is the mother of an adopted daughter from China.

Candace C. Crandall is an associate producer for New River Media Inc. and an adjunct fellow with the National Center for Public Policy Research in Washington, D.C. She has published more than two hundred articles, editorials and book reviews on public policy topics in publications such as the *Wall Street Journal, First Things,* the *Cleveland Plain Dealer,* the *Washington Times,* the *San Diego Union-Tribune* and the *Women's Quarterly.*

Paige Comstock Cunningham is a senior fellow at the Center for Bioethics and Human Dignity, a fellow at the Wilberforce Forum's Council for Biotechnology Policy, a fellow at the Institute for Biotechnology and the Human Future, an adjunct professor of law at Trinity Law School and an adjunct instructor at Wheaton College. Ms. Cunningham lectures and has published numerous articles, editorials and book chapters in the area of law and bioethics, has testified before congressional committees at the state and national level, and has appeared frequently on radio and television.

Jean Bethke Elshtain is the Laura Spelman Rockefeller Professor of Social and Political Ethics at the University of Chicago. She is the author of many works, including the feminist classic *Public Man, Private Woman: Women in Social and Political Thought; Jane Addams and the Dream of American Democracy;* and most recently, *Just War against Terror: The Burden of American Power in a Violent World* (Basic Books, 2003). Professor Elshtain currently serves as co-chair of the Pew Forum on Religion and American Public Life.

Serrin M. Foster is president of Feminists for Life of America. She is widely recognized as an international spokesperson for pro-life feminism, having lectured and moderated Pregnancy Resource Forums at top colleges across America, including Harvard, Stanford, Notre Dame and Texas A&M, and internationally at Oxford and Cambridge universities, among others. An earlier version of the chapter found in this volume was included in the anthology *Women's Rights,* edited by Jennifer Hurley, in a series entitled "Great Speeches in History," published by Greenhaven Press.

Elizabeth Fox-Genovese is the Eléonore Raoul Professor of the Humanities and professor of history at Emory University, where she was the founding director of the Institute for Women's Studies. She is the author of several books, including *Feminism without Illusions: A Critique of Individualism* and *"Feminism Is Not the Story of My Life": How Today's Feminist Elite Has Lost Touch with the Real Concerns of Women.* In 2003, Professor Fox-Genovese was awarded the National Humanities Medal. She currently serves on the President's Council on Bioethics and as editor for the *Journal of the Historical Society.*

Mary Ann Glendon is the Learned Hand Professor of Law at Harvard Law School. She is the author of numerous books, including *Rights Talk: The Impoverishment of Political Discourse; Abortion and Divorce in Western Law;* and most recently, *A World Made New: Eleanor Roosevelt and the Universal Declaration of Human Rights* (Random House, 2001). In 1998, the *National Law Journal* named Professor Glendon one of the "Fifty Most Influential Women Lawyers in America." She currently serves on the President's Council on Bioethics and is president of the Pontifical Academy for the Social Sciences.

Angela Lanfranchi is a clinical assistant professor of surgery at the Robert Wood Johnson Medical School, a co-founder of the Breast Cancer Prevention Institute, and a member of the Medical Expert Advisory Panel for the New Jersey State Board of Medical Examiners. Dr. Lanfranchi has lectured internationally on breast cancer risk and prevention to lay and medical audiences. In 2004, the Somerset County Commission on the Status of Women honored her for her contributions to women's health. Most recently, she has begun collaborating with breast cancer researchers at Fox Chase Cancer Center to discover the genomic basis for breast cancer.

Elizabeth R. Schiltz is an associate professor at the University of St. Thomas School of Law in Minneapolis, where she teaches in the areas of contract, commercial and banking law. Her most recent publication is "The Amazing, Elastic, Ever-Expanding Exportation Doctrine and Its Effect on Predatory Lending Regulation," published in 2004 in the *Minnesota Law Review*. She is currently writing an article on discrimination in lending against people with disabilities. Professor Schiltz is the mother of four children.

Elizabeth Shadigian is a clinical associate professor of obstetrics and gynecology at the University of Michigan. She is a fellow of the American College of Obstetricians and Gynecologists (ACOG) and is a board member and secretary of the American Association of Pro-Life Obstetricians and Gynecologists, a special interest group of ACOG. Her most recent publications include "Long Term Physical and Psychological Consequences of Induced Abortion: A Review of the Evidence," published in January 2003 in the *Obstetrics and Gynecology Survey*. Dr. Shadigian has written book chapters and speaks nationally on issues concerning abortion complications and violence against women.

Acknowledgments

ALL OF THE ESSAYS IN THIS COLLECTION, save one, were selected from papers presented at a series of symposia on the impact of abortion on women, organized and sponsored by the Women's Fund of Americans United for Life. These symposia, co-sponsored by Women Affirming Life and Feminists for Life of America, were held in November 2002 and January 2003 at Georgetown University, St. John's University and Boston College Law School. Presenters at the symposia included scholars at the nation's finest universities and think tanks, highly credentialed medical doctors and psychiatrists, practicing attorneys and columnists.

We gratefully acknowledge the financial support of the Pilgrim Foundation, which provided the critical initial funding for the symposia, as well as additional financial support from the Maclellan Foundation, the Link Foundation, the Crossed Foundation, the Hulseman Charitable Foundation, Thomas Haderlein, Preston and Nancy Athey, and an anonymous donor.

The editor also wishes to thank the following people for their generous assistance on this project: Dr. Vassilios Bezzerides, Dr. Greg Giugliano, Teresa Giugliano, Emily and Michael Marcucci, and Johanna Webber, for reading and providing helpful criticism of an early version of the manuscript; Doug Johnson for research support; Donna Harrison, Byron Calhoun and Marjorie Dannenfelser for their professional insight; Marianne Luthin for finding me; JME and BVM for their involvement; Peter Samuelson for his enthusiasm and determination; Clarke Forsythe for his consistent guidance, patience and trust; and Peter Collier and Loretta Barrett for their expertise, warmth and wit.

The eleven women who contributed to this volume are truly extraordinary, not only in the talent they display in their respective fields, but also in their humility, graciousness and gratitude. Thank you for your time and dedication to this project.

Finally, I wish to acknowledge my gratitude for my husband, Daniel Bachiochi, for his loving support, undying patience, and editorial insight during the editing and publication process. Without him, this book would never have come to be.

Notes

Part I. Abortion, Women and Culture

Chapter 1: From Culture Battles to Building a Culture of Life

1. This chapter was adapted from an essay that originally appeared in *First Things,* June/July 2003.
2. Louis Roussel, "Démographie: deux decennies de mutations dans les pays industrialisés," in *Family, State, and Economic Security,* vol. 1, ed. M. T. Meulders and J. Eekelaar (Brussels: Story Scientia, 1998), 27–41.
3. See generally Mary Ann Glendon, *Abortion and Divorce in Western Law* (Cambridge, Mass.: Harvard University Press, 1987).
4. Ibid.
5. See, for instance, John Hart Ely, "The Wages of Crying Wolf: A Comment on *Roe v. Wade,*" *Yale Law Journal* 82 (1973): 920.
6. Walker Percy, *The Thanatos Syndrome* (New York: Ballantine Books, 1987), 216.
7. Sandra Day O'Connor, *The Majesty of the Law: Reflections of a Supreme Court Justice* (New York: Random House, 2003), 45 ("Since the Court struck down as unconstitutional limitations by states on abortions in the first three months of pregnancy [citation to *Roe*], large numbers of people have taken regularly to the streets to demonstrate either their support of or their opposition to the decision.") and 244 ("When in the 1970s the Court struck down as unconstitutional limitations by states on abortions in the first

three months of pregnancy, a new body of protestors took to the
streets in opposition.").

[8] *Stenberg v. Carhart,* 530 U.S. 914 (2000).

[9] David M. Heer and Amyra Grossbard-Schechtman, "The Impact of
the Female Marriage Squeeze and the Contraceptive Revolution on
Sex Roles and the Women' s Liberation Movement in the United
States, 1960 to 1975," *Journal of Marriage and the Family,* February
1981: 49–65.

[10] Elizabeth Fox-Genovese, *"Feminism Is Not the Story of My Life": How
Today's Feminist Elite Has Lost Touch with the Real Concerns of
Women* (New York: Doubleday, 1996).

[11] National Institute of Allergy and Infectious Disease, *Fact Sheet,* July
1999.

[12] R. Herrero et al., "Human Papillomavirus and Oral Cancer," *Journal
of the National Cancer Institute* 2003:95: 1772–83.

[13] See Part II in this volume.

[14] See, for instance, CBS News/*New York Times* poll, January 2003;
Center for the Advancement of Women poll, 2003; Zogby Interna-
tional poll, November 2002; Gallup poll, May 2001; *Los Angeles
Times* poll, June 2000; CNN/*USA Today*/Gallup poll, July 1999;
Annual Survey of College Freshmen, January 1999, Higher Educa-
tion Research Institute, University of California at Los Angeles.

[15] Zogby International poll, November 2002; see also Annual Survey
of College Freshmen, January 1999, Higher Education Research
Institute; Harvard University's Institute of Politics poll, 2003;
Gallup Youth Survey, August 2003.

[16] Zogby International poll, November 2002, reported that first
among those adults who believe that abortion should never be
permitted are those ages 18–29.

[17] CNN/*USA Today*/Gallup poll, May 1999.

Chapter 2: Three Decades of Empty Promises

[1] This chapter was adapted from an essay that originally appeared in
First Things, January 2003.

[2] Centers for Disease Control, Morbidity and Mortality Weekly
Report, *Abortion Surveillance—United States, 2000* (November 28,
2003), 52(SS12): 1–32.

[3] Commission on Population Growth and America's Future, *Reports
Presented to President Richard M. Nixon,* May 5, 1972.

[4] Personal recollection by Candace Crandall of Los Angeles television news report, 1974.

[5] CBS TV program, *Maude,* "Maude's Dilemma," shown in two parts, November 14 and November 21, 1972.

[6] See, for instance, Jane Rosenzweig, "Can TV Improve Us?" *American Prospect,* July/August 1999.

[7] "Combating Out of Wedlock Births," *Family First,* November 1999.

[8] National Center for Health Statistics, *Fastats: Health, United States, 2003,* Table 9: Nonmarital Childbearing According to Race and Hispanic Origin of Mother and Maternal Age: United States, Selected Years 1970–2001, "all races and origins" and "black or African American."

[9] "Survey of Attitudes toward Elective Abortions," American College of Obstetricians and Gynecologists, 1985.

[10] "National Survey of Obstetricians/Gynecologists on Contraception and Unplanned Pregnancy: Attitudes and Practices with Regard to Abortion," Kaiser Family Foundation, 1995.

[11] "Supplement to the Monthly Vital Statistics Report: Advance Reports 1986: Series 24, Compilations of Data on Natality, Mortality, Marriage, Divorce, and Induced Terminations of Pregnancy, No. 3," *Vital and Health Statistics,* National Center for Health Statistics (CDC).

[12] National Vital Statistics Reports, vol. 48, no. 18, *United States Life Tables, 1998* (PHS) 2000-1120.

[13] Mary Calderone, "Illegal Abortion as Public Health Problem," *American Journal of Public Health* 50 (July 1960): 951.

[14] Susan Edmiston, "Report on the Abortion Capital of the Country," *New York Times Magazine,* April 11, 1971: SM10.

[15] *Chicago Sun Times* series, Section A, published November 13 through November 29, 1978, under various headlines.

[16] "Abortion Mills Thriving behind Secrecy and Fear," *New York Times,* November 24, 1991: A1.

[17] Anne Cowles, "Suit Names Doctors, Emory in Abortion Death," *Atlanta Journal-Constitution,* May 10, 1990; Jennifer Liebrum, "Abortion Doctor Has History of Suits," *Houston Chronicle,* November 7, 1991; "Doctor in Abortion Case Told to Pay $25 Million," Associated Press, January 30, 1991; Sandra Jacobs, "Infection Kills Abortion Patient," *Miami Herald,* February 7, 1996; Patricia Nealon and Judy Rakowsky, "Abortion Clinic's Testing Probed," *Boston Globe,* December 9, 1995; "Abortion Assembly Line Blamed in Death," *Los Angeles Times,* August 12, 1989; Andrew Fegelman, "Mom Sues Abortion Clinic after 13-Year-Old Girl Dies," *Chicago Tribune,* May 5, 1994; Lisa Belkin, "7 More Patients Accuse Doctor of Botching Their Abortions," *New York Times,* November 21, 1991.

[18] The federal Partial-Birth Abortion Ban Act of 2003 has been enjoined pending the outcome of three lawsuits filed by the National Abortion Federation, Planned Parenthood and the Center for Reproductive Rights in New York, California and Nebraska.

[19] A Citizen Petition that was filed on August 20, 2002, with the FDA describes the threat from RU-486 to women's health. The petition also delineates the procedural violations that occurred during the FDA's process of approving the abortion drug.

[20] "Abortion Can Take Tragic Toll on Women's Health," *Hamilton Spectator* (Canada), August 7, 2002: A11.

[21] Wirthlin Worldwide poll (1998), conducted for the Family Research Council, Washington, D.C.

[22] Annual Survey of College Freshmen, January 1999, Higher Education Research Institute, University of California at Los Angeles.

[23] *Los Angeles Times* poll, released June 18, 2000.

[24] Ibid.

[25] Centers for Disease Control, Morbidity and Mortality Weekly Report, *Abortion Surveillance—United States, 1995* (July 3, 1998), 47(SS02): 31–68. See also the Appendix to this volume.

[26] The Census Bureau confirmed data released by the National Center for Health Statistics on February 12, 2002, indicating that the U.S. birth rate stood at 2.1 per woman on average, the highest in 30 years.

Chapter 3: Coming of Age in a Culture of Choice

[1] Maggie Gallagher, *Enemies of Eros* (Chicago: Bonus Books, 1989), 116.

[2] Pierre Manent, "Modern Individualism," *A Free Society Reader,* ed. Michael Novak, William Brailsford and Cornelis Heesters (Maryland: Lexington Books, 2000), 213.

[3] See James Hitchcock, *American Culture and the Problem of Divorce* (Bronx: Fordham University Press, 1983); and Joseph Epstein, *Divorce in America* (New York: E. P. Dutton, 1974).

[4] See Judith Wallerstein, *The Unexpected Legacy of Divorce* (New York: Hyperion, 2000); and Patrick Fagan and Robert Rector, "The Effects of Divorce on America," *Heritage Foundation Backgrounder* no. 1373 (June 5, 2000).

[5] Aida Torres and J. D. Forrest, "Why Do Women Have Abortions?" *Family Planning Perspectives* 20:4 (July/August 1988): 170.

[6] Hadley Arkes, *Natural Rights and the Right to Choose* (New York: Cambridge University Press, 2002), 172.

[7] Sixteen states and the federal government have passed homicide

laws that recognize unborn children as victims throughout the entire period of prenatal development. Fifteen states' homicide laws recognize the unborn as victims through some specified part of the prenatal development period. *Crimes Against the Unborn Child Act: Fetal Homicide Model Legislation and Policy Guide,* Americans United for Life, March 2004.

[8] Minn. Stat. Ann. §§609.266, 609.2661–609.2665, 609.268(1) (West 1987).

[9] George Will, column, *Washington Post,* October 27, 2002.

[10] *Planned Parenthood of Southeastern Pennsylvania v. Casey,* 505 U.S. 833, 851 (1992).

[11] Wirthlin Worldwide poll (1998).

Chapter 4: The Feminist Case Against Abortion

[1] This chapter was adapted from an essay first presented at The Commonwealth Club of San Francisco.

[2] Mary Wollstonecraft, *A Vindication of the Rights of Woman* (Boston: Peter Edes, 1792).

[3] *The Revolution,* July 8, 1869, 4(1): 4.

[4] Elizabeth Cady Stanton to Julia Ward Howe, October 16, 1871, Julia Ward Howe diary, Harvard University Library.

[5] Personal conversation between Rosemary Bottcher and Bernard Nathanson, Denver, June 1986.

[6] Max Singer, "The Population Surprise," *Atlantic Monthly,* August 1999. "The rapid increase in population during the past two centuries has been the result of lower death rates, which have produced an increase in worldwide life expectancy from about thirty to about sixty-two.... But even during this population explosion the average number of children born to each woman—the fertility rate—has been falling in modernizing societies. The prediction that the world's population will soon begin to decline is based on almost universal behavior. In the United States fertility has been dropping for 200 years (except for the blip of the Baby Boom), but partly because of immigration it has stayed only slightly below replacement level."

[7] Conversation between Bottcher and Nathanson, 1986.

[8] Ibid.

[9] Bernard Nathanson, *Aborting America* (New York: Doubleday, 1979), 193.

[10] "Trends in Pregnancies and Pregnancy Rates by Outcome: Estimates for the United States, 1976–96," *Vital and Health Statistics,*

National Center for Health Statistics (CDC), vol. 21, no. 56 (PHS) 2000-1934.

11 "Facts in Brief: Induced Abortion," Alan Guttmacher Institute, 2003.

12 See, for instance, Maria Gallagher, "Abortionist with Checkered Past Opens Penn. Abortion Business," LifeNews.com, September 23, 2003.

Chapter 5: Living in the Shadow of Mönchberg

1 Arthur Kent, *The Death Doctors* (New English Library, 1974), 256; Henry Friedlander, *The Origins of Nazi Genocide: From Euthanasia to the Final Solution* (Chapel Hill: University of North Carolina Press, 1995), 92–93.

2 Robert J. Lifton, *The Nazi Doctors* (New York: Basic Books, 1986), 52, citing Secret Order, August 18, 1939, "Re, duty to report mal-formed, etc. newborns."

3 For general descriptions of the establishment and operations of these "killing centers," see ibid, 45–79; Friedlander, *The Origins of Nazi Genocide.*

4 "Signs on the road leading to Hadamar warned that the danger of epidemics prohibited entry, but the chimney's smoke and the smell made local inhabitants aware of the nature of the opera-tion." Friedlander, *The Origins of Nazi Genocide*, 93. "The heavy smoke from the crematory building is said to be visible over Hadamar every day." Lifton, *The Nazi Doctors*, 75. "[T]he citizens of Hadamar watch the smoke rise out of the chimney and are tor-tured with the ever-present thought of the poor sufferers, espe-cially when the nauseating odors carried by the wind offend their nostrils." Kent, *The Death Doctors*, 256, citing August 1941 letter from the Bishop of Limburg.

5 Kent, *The Death Doctors*, 256, citing August 1941 letter from the Bishop of Limburg.

6 This term is taken from the title of a book that was seminal in the development of Nazi Germany's killing programs, *Die Freigabe der Vernichtung lebensunwerten Leben* ("The Permission to Destroy Life Unworthy of Life"), published in 1920 by a law professor named Karl Binding and a professor of psychiatry named Alfred Hoche. The authors stressed the burden such lives imposed on society, in comparison with their worth. Lifton, *The Nazi Doctors*, 46–47; Friedlander, *The Origins of Nazi Genocide*, 14–16.

7 The statistics for age-related risks of having a baby with Down

Syndrome, as well as a succinct discussion of all the prenatal tests discussed in this essay, can be found in the American College of Obstetricians and Gynecologists' Patient Education Pamphlet #AP089 (August 1994).

8 *Roe v. Wade,* 410 U.S. 113 (1973); *Doe v. Bolton,* 410 U.S. 179 (1973).

9 Elizabeth Ring-Cassidy and Ian Gentles, *Women's Health after Abortion: The Medical and Psychological Evidence* (Toronto: The deVeber Institute for Bioethics and Social Research, 2002), 158. For an insightful critique of the "reassurance" rationale for prenatal testing, see Abby Lippman, "The Genetic Construction of Testing," in *Women and Prenatal Testing: Facing the Challenges of Genetic Technology,* ed. Karen H. Rothenberg and Elizabeth J. Thompson (Columbus: Ohio State University Press, 1994), 9.

10 Abby Lippman argues that "while a woman may have no control over or responsibility for the chromosomal occurrence of Down Syndrome, she can control the birth of a child with this condition by being tested. Thus, if a child with Down Syndrome is born to a woman who has refused testing, this becomes an event for which the child's mother is responsible because she could have prevented its occurrence. The individual is made into an agent of the state. . . . Prenatal testing . . . reshapes the problem of disability so that it need not be ours collectively to solve (what will we do to embrace and accommodate those among us with disabilities?), but becomes . . . one for the individual woman to prevent (what will she do to avoid having a baby with a disability?)" Lippman, "The Genetic Construction of Testing," 22–23.

11 *Sunday Times* (London), July 4, 1999, as reported in *American Feminist,* Winter 1999–2000: 22. For similar arguments, see the sources cited in Anne Kerr and Tom Shakespeare, *Genetic Politics: From Eugenics to Genome* (Cheltenham, U.K.: New Clarion Press, 2002), 143.

12 Larry Thompson, "The Price of Knowledge: Genetic Tests That Predict Dire Conditions Become a Two-Edged Sword," *Washington Post,* October 10, 1989: Z07.

13 Anthony J. Cousineau and Ronald M. Lauer, "Heart Disease and Children with Down Syndrome," in *Medical and Surgical Care for Children with Down Syndrome,* ed. D. C. Van Dyke, Philip Mattheis, Susan Schoon Eberly and Janet Williams (Bethesda, Md.: Woodbine House, 1995), 36–63 (40% of all children with Down Sydrome have heart defects); Alberto Rasore-Quartino, "The Present State of Medical Knowledge in Down Syndrome," in *Down*

Syndrome: A Review of Current Knowledge, ed. Jena Rondal, Juan Perera and Lynn Nadel (London: Whurr Publishers Ltd., 1999), 153, 154 (50%); Julie R. Korenbert, Gillian Barlow, Lora Salandanan, Pranay Bhattacharyya, Xiao-Ning Chen and Gary E. Lyons, "The Genetic Origins of Cognition and Heart Disease in Down Syndrome" in *Down Syndrome: Visions for the 21st Century,* ed. William I. Cohen, Lynn Nadel and Myra E. Madnick (New York: Wiley-Liss, 2002), 275, 281 (40–60%).

[14] James Meikle, "Down's Children Denied Heart Ops by Biased Doctors," *Guardian,* April 2, 2001; "Down's Children Missed Out on Ops," BBC News Online, April 2, 2001, available at: http://news.bbc.co.uk/1/low/health/1255881.stm.

[15] Amy Dockser Marcus, "Ensuring Your Baby Will Be Healthy: Embryo Screening Testing Gains in Popularity and Controversy; Choosing a Child's Gender," *Wall Street Journal,* July 25, 2002: D1; Aaron Zitner, "A Girl or Boy, You Pick," *Los Angeles Times,* July 23, 2002: A1.

[16] Garland E. Allen, "Is a New Eugenics Afoot?" *Science,* October 5, 2001: 59.

[17] One study calculated the lifetime cost to society of each child born with Down Syndrome to be $451,000. Another calculated the cost to be at least $1 million. Tucker Carlson, "Eugenics, American Style: The Abortion of Down Syndrome Babies," *Weekly Standard,* December 2, 1996: 20, 22–23.

[18] Zitner, "A Girl or Boy, You Pick," quoting Deborah Kaplan, executive director of the World Institute on Disability in Oakland, California. See also Kerr and Shakespeare, *Genetic Politics,* 143–45.

[19] Pearl S. Buck, *The Child Who Never Grew,* 2nd ed. (Bethesda, Md.: Woodbine House, 1992), 78.

[20] Edward J. Larson, *Sex, Race, and Science: Eugenics in the Deep South* (Baltimore: Johns Hopkins University Press, 1995), 167.

[21] I Corinthians 12:12, 17–22.

Chapter 6: Abortion: A War on Women

[1] This essay first appeared in *Touchstone: A Journal of Mere Christianity,* September 2003.

[2] Lawrence B. Finer and Stanley K. Henshaw, "Abortion Incidence and Services in the United States in 2000," *Perspectives on Sexual and Reproductive Health* 35:1 (2003): 6–15.

[3] "State Reports—New York: Provider Had History of Botching Abortions," *Kaiser Daily Reproductive Health Report,* August 8, 1995.

There have also been a number of stories on the Mafia's investment in abortion clinics. See Bob Jones, "Making a Killing," World on the Web 16:13 (April 7, 2001); and Phil Brennan, "Is the Mob Now Whacking the Unborn?" NewsMax.com, March 30, 2001.

⁴ See Chapters 7 and 8 in this volume.

⁵ Ibid.

⁶ David C. Reardon, *Aborted Women, Silent No More* (Springfield, Ill.: Acorn Books, 1987, 2002); and David C. Reardon and Theresa Burke, *Forbidden Grief: The Unspoken Pain of Abortion* (Springfield, Ill.: Acorn Books, 2002). See also, Elizabeth Ring-Cassidy and Ian Gentles, *Women's Health after Abortion: The Medical and Psychological Evidence* (Toronto: The deVeber Institute for Bioethics and Social Research, 2002); David C. Reardon, "The Duty to Screen: Clinical, Legal and Ethical Implications of Predictive Risk Factors of Post-Abortion Maladjustment," *Journal of Contemporary Health Law and Policy* 20:1 (2003): 33–114 (better screening and counseling methods at abortion clinics would help warn women who are at highest risk for suffering negative psychological reactions).

⁷ Reardon, *Aborted Women.*

⁸ Ibid.

⁹ "Black Americans to Hold March for Life in Birmingham," Concerned Women for America, October 3, 2002.

¹⁰ Centers for Disease Control, Morbidity and Mortality Weekly Report, *Abortion Surveillance—United States, 1999* (November 29, 2002), 51(SS09): 1–28.

¹¹ Ibid.

¹² Jennifer Roback Morse, "Aborting Child Protection: Does Planned Parenthood Oppose Child Abuse?" *National Review Online,* October 23, 2002; Charles A. Donovan, "Planned Parenthood: A Business That's Never Been Richer," *Focus on the Family,* February 4, 2003. Reportedly for financial as well as ideological reasons, Planned Parenthood also provides referrals for abortions (from which it profits), but not for adoptions (from which it does not). See, for instance, "Planned Parenthood: Abortion Not Adoption," at American Life League, and Patricia Pitkus Bainbridge, "A New Religion: An Analysis of Planned Parenthood Federation of America's Annual Report (2000–2001)," *Life Decisions International* 5:2 (Spring 2002). On Planned Parenthood's campaigns to encourage very young women (girls) to have abortions, see Joseph Farah, "Planned Parenthood on the Run," WorldNetDaily.com, May 30, 2002; Art Moore, "Abortionists Mum on Concealment Charges:

Refuse Response to WND on Allegations They Protect Sexual Predators," WorldNetDaily.com, May 31, 2002.

13 For a general discussion of these issues as well as specific evidence on the attitude of different groups toward abortion, see Elizabeth Fox-Genovese, *"Feminism Is Not the Story of My Life"*: *How Today's Feminist Elite Has Lost Touch with the Real Concerns of Women* (New York: Doubleday, 1996).

Part II. Abortion and Women's Health

Chapter 7: Reviewing the Evidence, Breaking the Silence

1 Portions of this material appear in various written forms similar to this chapter, especially in J. M. Thorp, K. E. Hartmann and E. M. Shadigian, "Long-term physical and psychological health consequences of induced abortion: A review of the evidence," *Obstet & Gynecol Survey* 58:1 (2003); and Elizabeth Shadigian, "Breaking the Silence: Long-Term Physical Complications of Induced Abortion," in *Back to the Drawing Board: The Future of the Pro-Life Movement,* ed. Teresa Wagner (South Bend, Ind.: St. Augustine's Press, 2003).

2 M. Wynn and A. Wynn, *Some Consequences of Induced Abortion to Children Born Subsequently,* London Foundation for Education and Research in Childbearing (London, 1972); "More on Koop's study of abortion," *Family Planning Perspectives* 22:1 (1990): 36–39.

3 Thorp et al. (2003).

4 Ibid., 81–84.

5 J. Brind et al., "Induced abortion as an independent risk factor for breast cancer: A comprehensive review and meta-analysis," *J Epidemiol & Community Health* 50 (1996): 481–96.

6 E. M. Shadigian and F. M. Wolf, "Breast cancer and spontaneous and induced abortion: A systematic review and meta-analysis" (in review).

7 Thorp et al. (2003).

8 M. McMahon et al., "Age at first birth and breast cancer risk," *Bull World Health Org* 43 (1970): 209–21.

9 Thorp et al. (2003).

10 Ibid.

11 P. Wingo et al., "The risk of breast cancer following spontaneous or induced abortion," *Cancer Causes & Control* 8 (1997): 93–108; L. Bartholomew and D. Grimes, "The alleged association between induced abortion and risk of breast cancer: Biology or bias?" *Obstet Gynecol Survey* 53:11 (1998): 708–14.

12 K. Michels and W. Willett, "Does induced or spontaneous abortion affect the risk of breast cancer?" *Epidemiology* 7:5 (1996): 521–28.

13 Brind et al. (1996).

14 Shadigian and Wolf (in review).

15 Brind et al. used older studies and translated non-English studies. They also did not exclude any studies and used a different statistical approach from the unpublished study. The unpublished study used exclusion criteria and only English-language studies.

16 Brind et al. (1996); Shadigian and Wolf (in review).

17 J. R. Daling et al., "Risk of breast cancer among young women: Relationship to induced abortions," *J Natl Cancer Inst* 86 (1994): 1584–92.

18 M. Melbye et al., "Induced abortion and the risk of breast cancer," *N Eng J Med* 336:2 (1997): 81–85.

19 J. R. Daling et al., "Risk of breast cancer among white women following induced abortion," *Am J Epidemiol* 144 (1996): 373–80.

20 Daling et al. (1994).

21 See Thorp et al. (2003): 33–35.

22 Ibid., 49–72, Table 4.

23 Ibid., 49, 57, 59, 60, 63, 64, 70–72; page numbers omitted from quotation. (Risk ratio elevation of 1.3 to 2.0).

24 M. Gissler, E. Hemminki and J. Lonnqvist, "Suicides after pregnancy in Finland, 1987–94. Register linkage study," *BMJ* 313 (1996): 1431–34.

25 D. C. Reardon et al., "Deaths associated with pregnancy outcome: A linkage based study of low income women," *Southern Med J* 95·8 (2002): 834–41.

26 M. Gissler et al., "Pregnancy-associated mortality after birth, spontaneous abortion, or induced abortion in Finland, 1987–2000," *Am J Obstet & Gynecol* 190 (2004): 422–27.

27 A. Gilcrest et al., "Termination of pregnancy and psychiatric morbidity," *Br J Psychiatry* 167 (1995): 243–48.

28 C. Morgan et al., "Suicides after pregnancy," letter, *BMJ* 314 (1997): 902.

29 H. W. Lawson et al., "Abortion mortality, United States, 1972 through 1987," *Am J Obstet & Gynecol* 171:5 (1994): 1365–72.

30 H. Atrash et al., "The relation between induced abortion and ectopic pregnancy," *Obstet & Gynecol* 89 (1997): 512–18.

31 Centers for Disease Control, Morbidity and Mortality Weekly Report, *Abortion Surveillance—United States, 1989–Present.*

32 Lawson et al. (1994).

33 Gissler et al. (1996); Reardon et al. (2002); Gissler et al. (2004).

34 Compendium of Selected Publications, the American College of Obstetricians and Gynecologists, Practice Bulletin #26 (2004).

Chapter 8: The Abortion–Breast Cancer Link

1 J. Brind et al., "Induced abortion as an independent risk factor for breast cancer: a comprehensive review and meta-analysis," *J Epidemiol & Community Health* 50 (1996): 481–96.

2 M. Melbye et al., "Induced abortion and the risk of breast cancer," *N Eng J Med* 336:2 (1997): 81–85.

3 Those studies that show a statistically significant link between abortion and breast cancer are as follows: M. Segi et al., "An epidemiological study on cancer in Japan," *GANN* 48 (Suppl) (1957): 1–63; L. Rosenberg et al., "Breast cancer in relation to the occurrence and time of induced and spontaneous abortion," *Am J Epidemiol* 127 (1988): 981–89; H. L. Howe et al., "Early abortion and breast cancer risk among women under age 40," *Int J Epidemiol* 18 (1989): 300–4; A. E. Laing et al., "Breast cancer risk factors in African-American women: The Howard University Tumor Registry experience," *J Natl Med Assoc* 85 (1993): 931–39; A. E. Laing et al., "Reproductive and lifestyle factors for breast cancer in African-American women," *Genet Epidemiol* 11 (1994): A300; J. R. Daling et al., "Risk of breast cancer among young women: relationship to induced abortions," *J Natl Cancer Inst* 86 (1994): 1584–92; J. R. Daling et al., "Risk of breast cancer among white women following induced abortion," *Am J Epidemiol* 144 (1996): 373–80; P. A. Newcomb et al., "Pregnancy termination in relation to risk of breast cancer," *JAMA* 275 (1996): 283–87; J. R. Palmer et al., "Induced abortion in relation to risk of breast cancer (United States)," *Cancer Causes Control* 8 (1997): 841–49; F. Nishiyama, "The epidemiology of breast cancer in Tokushima prefecture," *shikoku Ichi* 38 (1982): 333–43 (in Japanese); M. G. Le et al., "Oral contraceptive use and breast or cervical cancer: preliminary results of a French case-control study," in *Hormones and Sexual Factors in Human Cancer Aetiology*, ed. J. P. Wolff and J. S. Scott (Amsterdam: Elsevier, 1984), 139–47; L. Lipworth et al., "Abortion and the risk of breast cancer: a case-control study in Greece," *Int J Cancer* 61 (1995): 181–84; M. A. Rookus and F. E. van Leeuwen, "Induced abortion and risk for breast cancer: reporting (recall) bias in a Dutch case-control study," *J Natl Cancer Inst* 88 (1996): 1759–64; L. Bu et al., "Risk of breast cancer associated with induced abortion in a population at

low risk of breast cancer," *Am J Epidemiol* 141 (1995): S85 (abstract 337); R. Talamini et al., "The role of reproductive and menstrual factors in cancer of the breast before and after menopause," *Eur J Cancer* 32A (1996): 303–10; E. Luporsi (1988), in N. Andrieu et al., "Familial risk, abortion and their interactive effect on the risk of breast cancer: a combined analysis of six case-control studies," *Br J Cancer* 72 (1995): 744–51; T. E. Rohan (1988) in Andrieu et al. (1995).

4   Daling et al. (1994); Melbye et al. (1997).
5   Daling et al. (1994).
6   B. E. Henderson, R. Ross and L. Bernstein, "Estrogen is a cause of human cancer: The Richard and Hilda Rosenthal Foundation Award Lecture." *Cancer Research* 48 (1988): 246–53.
7   Katherine Miller, "Estrogen and DNA damage: the silent source of breast cancer?" *J Natl Cancer Inst* 95 (2003): 100–2.
8   Writing group for the Women's Health Initiative Investigators, "Risks and benefits of estrogen plus progestin in healthy postmenopausal women," *JAMA* 288 (2002): 321–33.
9   Collaborative Group on Hormonal Factors in Breast Cancer, "Breast cancer and hormonal contraceptives: collaborative reanaly-sis of individual data on 53,297 women with breast cancer and 100,239 women without breast cancer from 54 epidemiologic studies," *Lancet* 47 (1996): 1713–27.
10 Diagrams modified from I. H. Russo and J. Russo, "Mammary gland neoplasia in long-term rodent studies," *Env Health Persp* 104 (1996): 938–67.
11 J. Russo, L. K. Tay and I. H. Russo, "Differentiation of the mam-mary gland and susceptibility to carcinogenesis," *Breast Cancer Res & Treatment* 2 (1982): 5–73.
12 Daling et al. (1994); Russo et al. (1982).
13 M. Melbye et al., "Preterm delivery and risk of breast cancer," *Brit J Cancer* 80 (1999): 609. In contrast, pregnancies that result in first-trimester spontaneous abortions (i.e., miscarriages) produce sub-normal estrogen concentrations and generally *do not* increase breast cancer risk. That is, there is little estrogen stimulation of the breast. D. R. Stewart et al., "Enhanced ovarian steroid secretion before implantation in early human pregnancy," *J Clin Endocrinol Metab* 76 (1993): 1470–76; J. Kunz and P. J. Keller, "HCG, HPL, oestradiol, progesterone and AFP in serum in patients with threat-ened abortion," *Br J Obstet Gynaecol* 83 (1976): 640–44; B. R. Witt et al., "Relaxin, CA-125, progesterone, estradiol, Schwangerschaft

protein, and human chorionic gonadotropin as predictors of outcome in threatened and non-threatened pregnancies," *Fertil Steril*
53 (1990): 1029–36; R. J. Norman et al., "Inhibin and relaxin concentrations in early singleton, multiple, and failing pregnancy:
relationship to gonadotropin and steroid profiles," *Fertil Steril* 59
(1993): 130–37.

[14] DMBA is the short form of Dimethylbenzanthracene.

[15] J. Russo and I. H. Russo, "Susceptibility of the mammary gland to
carcinogenesis II: pregnancy interruption as a risk factor in tumor
incidence," *Am J Pathol* 100 (1980): 497–512.

[16] Daling et al. (1994); Lipworth et al. (1995).

[17] Melbye et al. (1997).

[18] Abortion was liberalized in Denmark in 1956 and again in the
1970s. M. Osler et al., "Family planning services delivery," *Dan
Med Bull* 37 (1990): 96–104.

[19] Collaborative Group on Hormonal Factors in Breast Cancer,
"Breast cancer and abortion: collaborative reanalysis of data from
53 epidemiological studies, including 83,000 women with breast
cancer from 16 countries," *Lancet* 363 (2004): 1007–16.

[20] "Study: Breast Cancer Not Tied to Abortion," *Atlanta Journal-
Constitution*, March 26, 2004.

[21] The four studies not mentioned in the Beral et al. analysis were:
Laing et al. (1994); Bu et al. (1995); Luporsi (1988) in Andrieu et al.
(1995); D. G. Zaridze (1995) in Andrieu et al. (1995).

[22] Melbye et al. (1997); M. J. Goldacre et al., "Abortion and breast
cancer: a case-control record linkage study," *J Epidemiol & Community Health* 55 (2001): 336–37; G. Erlandsson et al., "Abortions and
breast cancer: record-based case-control study," *Int J Cancer* 103
(2003): 676–79.

[23] See generally John Kindley, "The fit between the elements for an
informed consent cause of action and the scientific evidence linking induced abortion with increased breast cancer risk," *Wisconsin
Law Review* 1998:6 (1998): 1595 ("the current level of scientific
evidence linking induced abortion with increased breast cancer risk
is sufficient to support an ethical and legal duty to disclose fully the
risk to women who are considering pregnancy termination").

[24] Stuart Donnan, "Abortion, breast cancer, and impact factors—in
this number and the last," *J Epidemiol & Community Health* 50
(1996): 605.

[25] Dr. Lanfranchi would like to thank Dr. Joel Brind for his significant
contributions to this chapter.

Chapter 9: The Psychological Aftermath of Three Decades of Abortion

1. Jeremiah 31:15.
2. Melinda Tankard Reist, *Giving Sorrow Words* (Sydney: Duffy & Snell-grove, 2000).
3. M. C. Freda et al., "The lived experience of miscarriage after infertility," *American Journal of Maternal/Child Nursing* 28:1 (2003): 16–23.
4. Ibid.
5. Reist, *Giving Sorrow Words*, 17.
6. Ibid., 20.
7. Ibid., 90.
8. Beverly Raphael, *The Anatomy of Bereavement* (New York: Basic Books, 1983), 238.
9. Reist, *Giving Sorrow Words*, 40.
10. Ibid., 40–41.
11. Ibid., 41.
12. Ibid., 13.
13. Ibid., 21.
14. The Federal Document Clearing House, *President Clinton Makes Remarks upon Vetoing Partial-Birth Abortion Bill*, transcript, April 10, 1996.
15. See B. Calhoun et al., "Comprehensive care for the family of the fetus with a lethal condition," *J Reproductive Med* 48 (2003): 343–48 ("It appears that when parents are given comprehensive, multidisciplinary, individualized and informed counsel, including clinical expectations, in the setting of a lethal fetal condition, they frequently choose the option of perinatal hospice care for the management of pregnancy."); N. Hoeldtke and B. Calhoun, "Perinatal hospice," *Am J Obstet & Gynecol* 185 (2001): 525–29.
16. Reist, *Giving Sorrow Words*, 4–5.
17. Vincent Rue, *Forgotten Fathers*, pamphlet (Lewiston, N.Y.: Life Cycle Books, 1997).
18. *Planned Parenthood v. Casey*, 505 U.S. 833, 898 (1992).
19. M. Gissler et al., "Suicides after pregnancy in Finland, 1987–94: register linkage study," *BMJ* 313 (1996): 1431–34.
20. P. K. Coleman et al., "State funded abortions versus deliveries: a comparison of outpatient mental health claims over 4 years," *Am J Orthopsychiatry* 73:1 (2002): 141–52.
21. D. C. Reardon et al., "Deaths associated with pregnancy outcome: a record linkage study of low income women," *Southern Med J* 95:8 (2002): 834–41.

22 Pope John Paul II, *Evangelium Vitae: The Gospel of Life* (1997), para. 99.

23 Ibid.

24 Pope John Paul II, *On the Christian Meaning of Human Suffering* (February 11, 1984), para. 30.

Part III. Abortion, Law, Regulation and Alternatives

Chapter 10: The Supreme Court and the Creation of the Two-Dimensional Woman

1 Justices Blackmun, Brennan, Powell and Marshall joined the Opinion of the Court; Justices Burger, Douglas and Stewart concurred in the judgment. Justices Rehnquist and White dissented.

2 *Doe v. Bolton,* 410 U.S. 179, 222 (Justice White, dissenting).

3 Ibid., 152.

4 Ibid.

5 Ibid., 153.

6 Ibid., 164 (emphasis added).

7 Ibid., 166 (emphasis added).

8 Ibid., 162.

9 Ibid., 165.

10 Ibid., 163.

11 Ibid., 192.

12 Ibid., 153.

13 Gerard V. Bradley, "Reversing *Roe*," in *Building a Culture of Life: 30 Years after Roe v. Wade,* ed. William L. Saunders and Brian C. Robertson (Washington, D.C.: Family Research Council, 2002), 13.

14 A controversial paper in 2000 argued that legalized abortion has contributed "significantly" to a drop in crime. John J. Donohue and Steven D. Levitt, "The Impact of Legalized Abortion on Crime," Berkeley Olin Program in Law and Economics, Working Paper Series, University of California at Berkeley, 2000. Not surprisingly, this reduction was cited with approval by Planned Parenthood as one of the "benefits" of legalized abortion. Another supposed "benefit" is the availability of abortion for parents who conceive a child with genetic disorders: "Fact Sheet: Medical and Social Health Benefits since Abortion Was Made Legal in the U.S.," Planned Parenthood website at: www.plannedparenthood.org/library/ABORTION/HealthBenef.html.

15 Caroline Whitbeck, "Taking Women Seriously as People" in *The Abortion Controversy: 25 Years after Roe v. Wade,* ed. Louis P. Pojman

and Francis J. Beckwith (Belmont, Calif.: Wadsworth Publishing Company, 1998): 434.

16 Ibid., 443 (emphasis in original).

17 *Doe v. Bolton,* 410 U.S. at 208 (Burger, C.J., concurring).

18 *Bigelow v. Virginia,* 421 U.S. 809 (1975).

19 *Planned Parenthood of Central Missouri v. Danforth,* 428 U.S. 52 (1976).

20 Ibid.

21 Ibid.

22 Ibid.

23 *Colautti v. Franklin,* 439 U.S. 379 (1979).

24 *Thornburgh v. American College of Obstetricians and Gynecologists,* 476 U.S. 747 (1986).

25 *City of Akron v. Akron Center for Reproductive Health,* 462 U.S. 416 (1983).

26 *Thornburgh,* 476 U.S. 747.

27 *City of Akron,* 462 U.S. 416.

28 *Planned Parenthood Association of Kansas City, Mo., v. Ashcroft,* 462 U.S. 476 (1983).

29 *Bellotti v. Baird (II),* 443 U.S. 622 (1979).

30 *Harris v. McRae,* 448 U.S. 297 (1980). The companion case, *Williams v. Zbaraz,* 448 U.S. 358 (1980), upheld the same freedom for states to limit Medicaid funding of abortion.

31 *Maher v. Roe,* 432 U.S. 464 (1977) (Connecticut excluded all but "medically necessary" abortions); *Beal v. Doe,* 432 U.S. 438 (1977) (Pennsylvania law with similar limitation); *Poelker v. Doe,* 432 U.S. 519 (1977) (St. Louis ban against abortions in public hospitals).

32 *Webster v. Reproductive Health Services,* 492 U.S. 490 (1989).

33 *Rust v. Sullivan,* 500 U.S. 173 (1991).

34 *People v. Campos,* 592 N.E.2d 85 (Ill. App. 1 Dist. 1992). Subsequent history: *appeal denied,* 602 N.E.2d 460 (Ill. 1992), *habeas corpus denied,* 827 F.Supp. 1359 (N.D. Ill. 1993), *affirmed,* 7 F.3d 1501 (7th Cir. 1994), *certiorari denied,* 514 U.S. 1024 (1995).

35 The Unborn Victims of Violence Act of 2004 passed with bipartisan support of the Congress and was signed by President Bush on April 1, 2004.

36 H.R. 2175 was signed by President Bush on August 5, 2002.

37 *Hope v. Perales,* 83 N.Y.2d 563, 634 N.E.2d 183, 611 N.Y.S.2d 811 (1994).

38 "HHS to Allow States to Provide SCHIP [*sic*] Coverage for Prenatal Care," Health and Human Services Press Release, January 31, 2002.

[39] Clarence Page, "Playing Politics with Prenatal Care," *St. Louis Post-Dispatch,* February 5, 2002.

[40] Jefferson Morley, "Fetal Mistake: The Abortion Rights Crowd Squanders a Victory," *Slate,* February 14, 2002 (quoting, first, Bob Herbert of the *New York Times,* and former surgeon general Jocelyn Elders).

[41] 45 C.F.R. Sec. 46.201–46.207 ("Additional Protections for Pregnant Women, Human Fetuses and Neonates Involved in Research") (2001).

[42] See Scott Rae, "The Ethics of Fetal Tissue Transplantation," *Christian Research Journal,* Fall 1991: 28.

[43] For an examination of every state and federal case citing *Roe* from 1973 to 1993, and supporting this conclusion, see Paul Benjamin Linton, *"Planned Parenthood v. Casey:* The Flight from Reason in the Supreme Court," *St. Louis University Public Law Review* 13 (1993): 15–136.

[44] See, e.g., Paige Cunningham and Clarke Forsythe, "Is Abortion the 'First Right' for Women?" in *Abortion, Medicine and the Law,* 4th ed., ed. J. Douglas Butler and David F. Walbert (New York: Facts on File, Inc., 1992), 100–58.

[45] The opinion begins: "Liberty finds no refuge in a jurisprudence of doubt. Yet, 19 years after our holding that the Constitution protects a woman's right to terminate her pregnancy in its early stages, that definition of liberty is still questioned." *Planned Parenthood v. Casey,* 505 U.S. at 833.

[46] *Planned Parenthood v. Casey,* 505 U.S. at 996.

[47] For a detailed analysis of *Casey,* comparing and contrasting it with *Roe,* see Linton, *"Planned Parenthood v. Casey."*

[48] The joint opinion iterated an "undue burden" standard. It explained that if a regulation "has the purpose or effect of placing a substantial obstacle in the path of a woman seeking an abortion of a nonviable fetus," it is an undue burden. *Planned Parenthood v. Casey,* 505 U.S. at 877. Of course, this is a tautology. Isn't "substantial obstacle" just another way of saying "undue burden?" The utter unworkability of this doctrine was made evident in *Stenberg v. Carhart,* where the Court struck down a Nebraska ban on partial-birth abortions. *Stenberg v. Carhart,* 530 U.S. 914 (2001). Two drafters of the undue-burden standard—O'Connor and Souter—joined the majority. Justice Kennedy, the third author of the joint opinion, dissented, concluding that Nebraska's law did not place an undue burden since it did not deny any women access to a safe

abortion. 530 U.S. at 965, 967. Justice O'Connor separately wrote that the statute posed an undue burden since it could be interpreted—despite Nebraska's assurances to the contrary—as covering more than one type of procedure. Justice Ginsburg, concurring, seemed taken by the notion that legislatively expressed distaste for abortion is an undue burden. Justice Stevens ignored the standard altogether, writing that it was "simply irrational" for the state to ban one "gruesome" late-term abortion procedure (partial-birth abortion) and not the other (dilation and evacuation, or D&E). 530 U.S. at 946–47. Justice Thomas, dissenting, was adamant about the problems with the *Casey* rule:

> Today's decision is so obviously irreconcilable with *Casey*'s explication of what its undue-burden standard requires, let alone the Constitution, that it should be seen for what it is, a reinstitution of the pre-*Webster* abortion-on-demand era in which the mere invocation of "abortion rights" trumps any contrary societal interest. If this statute is unconstitutional under *Casey*, then *Casey* meant nothing at all, and the Court should candidly admit it.
>
> 530 U.S. at 983.

He concluded:

> Under *Casey*, the regulation before us today should easily pass constitutional muster. But the Court's abortion jurisprudence is a particularly virulent strain of constitutional exegesis. And so today we are told that 30 States are prohibited from banning one rarely used form of abortion that they believe to border on infanticide.
>
> 530 U.S. at 1020.

Chief Justice Rehnquist joined Kennedy's and Thomas's dissents, writing that they "correctly applied *Casey*'s principles." Finally, in his dissent, Justice Scalia wrote that *Stenberg* was not a misapplication of *Casey*'s rule, but its "logical and entirely predictable consequence." 530 U.S. at 954. He stated that an undue burden is

> a value judgment, dependent upon how much one respects (or believes society ought to respect) the life of a partially delivered fetus, and how much one respects (or believes society ought to respect) the freedom of the woman who gave it life to kill it.... It has been arrived at by precisely the process *Casey* promised—a democratic vote by nine lawyers ... upon the pure policy question whether this limitation upon abortion is "undue"—*i.e.*, goes too far.
>
> 530 U.S. at 954–55.

49   Has there been a measurable decrease in the rates of illegitimacy, domestic violence, child abuse and female poverty? In 1993, William Bennett published his *Index of Leading Cultural Indicators*. He found an "alarming social regression" from the period 1960–1990. During that thirty-year period, he wrote, "there has been a 560% increase in violent crime; a 419% increase in illegitimate births; a quadrupling in divorce rates; a tripling of the percentage of children living in single-parent homes; more than a 200% increase in the teenage suicide rate; and a drop of almost 80 points in SAT scores." During the 1970s, illegitimacy increased from 10.7% in 1970, to 18.4% in 1980. The number of children living with single mothers grew by the same percentage, from 11% in 1970, to 18% in 1980. William J. Bennett, "Quantifying America's Decline," *Wall Street Journal,* March 15, 1993.

50   *Planned Parenthood v. Casey,* 505 U.S. at 855.

51   Ibid., 856.

52   Ibid., 860.

53   Ibid.

54   Ibid., 856.

55   Ibid., 956–57 (Rehnquist, C.J., dissenting).

56   Jennifer C. Braceras, "June Cleaver Wants Flex Time," Independent Women's Forum, Summer 2001.

57   Ibid.

58   Ibid.

59   Jerry Zremski, "Attitudes Becoming More Negative on Abortion," *Buffalo News* (New York), November 25, 2002: A1.

60   Ibid.

61   Fred Barnes, "Safe, Legal and Stigmatized," *Weekly Standard,* February 3, 2003.

62   Zremski, "Attitudes Becoming More Negative on Abortion."

63   Cheryl Wetzstein, "New Poll Shows Tilt to Protect Unborn," *Washington Times,* January 16, 2003.

64   Zremski, "Attitudes Becoming More Negative on Abortion."

65   Natalie Clarke, "Abortion Backlash," *Daily Mail* (London), March 13, 2003: 54.

66   Gallup Youth Survey, 2003.

67   Zremski, "Attitudes Becoming More Negative on Abortion." See also Sara Kugler, "US Abortion Rate Drops Significantly, Particularly among Teens," Associated Press, October 8, 2002. The CDC reports a rate of 17 per 1,000 for the same time period, explaining the difference as due to four nonreporting states with "relatively

high abortion rates." Centers for Disease Control, Morbidity and Mortality Weekly Report, *Abortion Surveillance—United States, 1999* (November 29, 2002), 51(SS09): 1–28.

68 Patricia Dalton, "Daughter of the Revolution," *Washington Post*, May 21, 2000.

69 Carolyn Graglia, *Domestic Tranquility* (Dallas: Spence Publishing Company, 1998), 193 (emphasis added).

70 Mary Cunningham Agee, "From Tears to Joy: How My Miscarriage Birthed a Ministry to Unwed Mothers," *Today's Christian Woman*, November/December 1997.

71 Frederica Mathewes-Green, *Real Choices* (Sisters, Ore.: Multnomah Books, 1994), 183.

72 *Planned Parenthood v. Casey*, 505 U.S. at 852.

73 Ibid., 851.

74 Ibid., 898.

75 Ibid.

76 The singular case of John Stachokus and Tanya Meyers is notorious for its unique, brief recognition of the father's interests. Judge Conahan granted a TRO to prevent John Stachokus' girlfriend from getting an abortion, so he could hear from both parties. Marie McCullough, "Court Injunction Halts Pa. Woman's Abortion," *Philadelphia Inquirer*, August 2, 2002.

77 Geraldine Sealey, "Duped Dads: Men Fight Centuries-Old Paternity Laws," ABC News, February 10, 2002.

78 The Texas House State Affairs Committee heard testimony about how abortion providers coach teens to avoid parental involvement. Janet Elliott, "Loopholes Found in Abortion Law," *Houston Chronicle*, April 8, 2003.

79 K. McDonnell, *Not an Easy Choice: A Feminist Re-examines Abortion* (Toronto: The Women's Press, 1984), 59 (citing M. Zimmerman, *Passage through Abortion: The Personal and Social Reality of Women's Experiences* (Westport, Conn.: Greenwood Publishing Group: 1977).

80 Sue Nathanson, *Soul Crisis: One Woman's Journey through Abortion to Renewal* (New York: Signet, 1990), 25, 41.

81 Elizabeth Kristol, "Picture Perfect: The Politics of Prenatal Testing," *First Things* 32 (April 1993): 22 (emphasis in original).

82 Lori Andrews, *Future Perfect: Confronting Decisions about Genetics* (New York: Columbia University Press, 2001), 63.

83 Kristol, "Picture Perfect," 22.

84 Andrews, *Future Perfect*, 63 (quoting geneticist Angus Clarke; endnote omitted).

[85] Barbara Katz Rothman, *The Tentative Pregnancy: How Amniocentesis Changes the Experience of Motherhood* (New York: W. W. Norton & Company, 1993).

[86] Andrews, *Future Perfect,* 57.

[87] Andrews relates the story of Kim Roembach-Ratliff. When she "learned through prenatal testing that her newborn child had spina bifida, her insurer wouldn't provide coverage for the child, saying that the disorder should be treated as a preexisting condition.... Roembach-Ratliff says, 'This genetic information was used against us.'" Andrews, *Future Perfect,* 133 (endnote omitted).

[88] Ibid., 100–1 (quoting NIH report; endnote omitted).

[89] Kristol, "Picture Perfect," 24.

[90] Jessica Hopp and Greg Sandoval, "Mystics Coach Was Cited in Pregnancy Suit," *Washington Post,* September 16, 2002.

[91] Matthew Cella, "Action Sought in Abortion Advice," *Washington Times,* August 13, 2002; Matthew Cella, "EMT Chief Linked to Abortions Retires," *Washington Times,* September 23, 2002.

[92] Martin, "Women Given Cruelest Choice Now Fight Back," *New York Times,* October 21, 1989: A27. See also *New York Daily News,* May 24, 1989. More than a dozen women claimed they were told to have abortions or resign their jobs. One miscarried, although she pleaded with her supervisor to allow her to see a doctor. Another who became pregnant was told to "stay home and collect (welfare) checks or get rid of it."

[93] Klebanoff, Shiono and Rhoads, "Outcomes of Pregnancy in a National Sample of Resident Physicians," *New England Journal of Medicine* 323 (1990): 1040–41.

[94] Ibid., 1030.

[95] Stern, "Female Talent at Law Firms," *National Law Journal,* March 18, 1991: 15–16.

Chapter 11: Abortion Clinic Regulation: Combating the True "Back Alley"

[1] Dial, "Abortion: A Dirty Industry," *Citizen Magazine,* July 2001.

[2] News, WAFB, Baton Rouge, Louisiana, February 4, 1999; Executive Order MJF 995, *Declaration of Public Health and Safety Emergency,* dated February 5, 1999 (signed by Governor Mike Foster).

[3] Dial, "Abortion: A Dirty Industry."

[4] Phoenix Police Department Report, dated July 15, 1998; testimony of Dr. John I. Biskind, *State v. Biskind,* no. CR99-00198 (Ariz. Superior Ct.), dated February 13, 2001.

⁵ M. Paul, E. Lichtenberg, L. Borgatta, D. Grimes and P. Stubblefield, *A Clinician's Guide to Medical and Surgical Abortion* (1999), 20–21.

⁶ Ibid., 197–98.

⁷ Ibid.

⁸ "Facts in Brief: Induced Abortion," The Alan Guttmacher Institute (January 2003).

⁹ "State Policies in Brief: Abortion Reporting Requirements," The Alan Guttmacher Institute (October 2002).

¹⁰ Ibid.

¹¹ Warren M. Hern, *Abortion Practice* 101 (1990).

¹² The following states regulate, in some manner and to some degree, the provision of all abortions: Alabama, Arizona, Arkansas, Connecticut, Florida, Georgia, Illinois, Kentucky, Louisiana, Michigan, Mississippi, Missouri, Nebraska, North Carolina, Oklahoma, Pennsylvania, Rhode Island, South Carolina, Texas and Wisconsin. Meanwhile, Alaska, California and Tennessee have laws regulating the provision of all abortions, but those laws are not enforced because the state attorney general has issued an opinion against enforcement.

¹³ The following states require that certain, primarily later-term, abortions be performed in hospitals: Massachusetts, New York, Ohio, Pennsylvania and Utah. The constitutionality of such a requirement is questionable, however. Similar requirements in Alaska, Hawaii, Idaho, Missouri, North Dakota, Oklahoma, South Dakota and Tennessee have been declared unconstitutional or rendered unenforceable by an opinion issued by the state attorney general.

¹⁴ The following states regulate only the provision of second-trimester abortions: Indiana, Minnesota, New Jersey, South Dakota, Utah and Virginia.

¹⁵ *Planned Parenthood of Southeastern Pennsylvania v. Casey*, 505 U.S. 833, 852 (1992).

¹⁶ Ibid.

¹⁷ *Greenville Women's Clinic v. Bryant*, 222 F.3d 157, 173 (4th Cir. 2000), *certiorari denied*, 531 U.S. 1191 (2001).

¹⁸ See e.g. Ariz. Admin. Code 9-10-1506(B)(2): "A physician with admitting privileges at an accredited hospital in this state is in the physical facilities until each patient is stable and ready to leave the recovery room."

¹⁹ From court documents and pleadings, it is clear that many abortion providers object to these industry standards—standards the

abortion industry (as a whole) has produced and many individual clinics and providers already implement (at least in part)—being mandatory and to providers being subject to criminal and civil penalties for not complying with the standards.

20 See e.g. *Hallmark Clinic v. North Carolina Dept. of Human Res.*, 380 F.Supp. 1153 (1974); *Friendship Medical Center Ltd. v. Chicago Board of Health*, 505 F.2d 1141 (7th Cir. 1974), *certiorari denied*, 420 U.S. 997 (1975); and *Mahoning Women's Center v. Hunter*, 619 F.2d 456, 460 (1979) (Ohio).

21 *Planned Parenthood of Southeastern Pennsylvania v. Casey*, 505 U.S. 833, 874–76 (1992).

22 For example, in the litigation surrounding the Arizona abortion clinic regulations, *Tucson Woman's Clinic v. Eden*, no. CIV 00-141-TUC-RCC (D. Ariz. Oct. 1, 2002), abortion providers complained about being required to employ nurses or physician assistants to monitor patient recovery rather than use inadequately trained, inexperienced and relatively low-paid medical assistants. The main complaint was the increased cost of a nurse or physician assistant. Abortion providers seemingly gave little or no consideration to the immense benefits that such personnel offer to patients.

23 The U.S. Constitution "commands that no State shall 'deny to any person within its jurisdiction the equal protection of the laws,' which is essentially a direction that all persons similarly situated should be treated alike." *City of Cleburne v. Cleburne Living Ctr. Inc.*, 473 U.S. 432, 439 (1985) (quoting *Plyler v. Doe*, 457 U.S. 202, 216 (1982)).

24 In recent litigation, abortion providers have argued that subjecting their clinics and offices to routine inspections to ensure compliance with standards mandated by the state's abortion clinic regulations violates their right to be free from "unreasonable searches and seizures." Specifically, they argue that state health department inspectors should not be allowed to inspect the clinics or offices (for compliance or in response to a complaint) without a judicial or administrative warrant issued by a state judge or magistrate. See e.g. *Tucson Woman's Clinic v. Eden*, no. CIV 00-141-TUC-RCC (D. Ariz. October 1, 2002).

25 See generally *Tucson Woman's Clinic v. Eden*, no. CIV 00-141-TUC-RCC (D. Ariz. Oct. 1, 2002); *Greenville Women's Clinic v. Bryant*, 222 F.3d 157 (4th Cir. 2000), *certiorari denied*, 531 U.S. 1191 (2001); *Greenville Women's Clinic v. Com'r, S.C. Dep't of Health and Environmental Control*, 306 F.3d 141 (4th Cir. 2002), *certiorari. denied*, 123

S.Ct. 1908 (U.S. 2003); *Women's Medical Center of Northwest Houston v. Bell*, 248 F.3d 411 (5th Cir. 2001); and *Women's Medical Center of Northwest Houston v. Bell*, Order, Civil Action no. H-99-3639 (S.D. Tex. April 1, 2002).

26 See e.g. *Greenville Women's Clinic v. Bryant*, 222 F.3d 157 (4th Cir. 2000), *certiorari denied*, 531 U.S. 1191 (2001); *Greenville Women's Clinic v. Com'r, S.C. Dep't of Health and Environmental Control*, 306 F.3d 141 (4th Cir. 2002); *Medical Center of Northwest Houston v. Bell*, 248 F.3d 411 (5th Cir. 2001); and *Tucson Woman's Clinic v. Eden*, no. CIV 00-141-TUC-RCC (D. Ariz. Oct. 1, 2002).

27 See *Greenville Women's Clinic v. Bryant*, 222 F.3d 157 (4th Cir. 2000), *certiorari denied*, 531 U.S. 1191 (2001).

28 Ibid.

29 *Greenville Women's Clinic v. Com'r, S.C. Dep't of Health and Environmental Control*, 306 F.3d 141 (4th Cir. 2002).

30 Ibid.

31 *Greenville Women's Clinic v. Com'r, S.C. Dep't of Health*, 123 S. Ct. 1908 (U.S. 2003).

32 See *Women's Medical Center of Northwest Houston v. Bell*, 248 F.3d 411 (5th Cir. 2001).

33 See *Women's Medical Center of Northwest Houston v. Bell*, Order, Civil Action No. H-99-3639 (S.D. Tex. April 1, 2002).

34 See *Tucson Woman's Clinic v. Eden*, Nos. 02-17375, 02-17381 and 02-17382 (9th Cir.).

35 See *Tucson Woman's Clinic v. Eden*, No. CIV 00-141-TUC-RCC, slip opinion p. 19 (D. Ariz. Oct. 1, 2002).

Chapter 12: Abortion-Alternative Legislation and the Law of the Gift

1 Galina Espinoza et al., "Small Blessings," *People*, February 25, 2002: 48.

2 Dave Clark, "Free Abortions Offered in NYC," *Family News in Focus* (October 5, 2001).

3 Pope John Paul II, *Evangelium Vitae: The Gospel of Life* (1997), para. 99.

4 Pastoral Constitution on the Church in the Modern World, *Gaudium et Spes* (1965), para. 24 ("This likeness reveals that man, who is the only creature on earth which God willed for itself, cannot fully find himself except through a sincere gift of himself (cf. Lk 17:33)."); *see also* John Paul II, *On the Dignity and Vocation of Women*, Apostolic Letter (August 15, 1988), para. 7 & 18 ("To be

human means to be called to interpersonal communion."); John Paul II, *Centesimus Annus,* Encyclical Letter (May 1, 1991), para. 41 ("When man does not recognize in himself and in others the value and grandeur of the human person, he effectively deprives himself of the possibility of benefiting from his humanity and of entering into that relationship of solidarity and communion with others for which God created him. Indeed, it is through the free gift of self that man truly finds himself.").

5   *Planned Parenthood of Southeastern Pennsylvania v. Casey,* 505 U.S. 833, 856 (1992) ("The ability of women to participate equally in the economic and social life of the Nation has been facilitated by their ability to control their reproductive lives.").

6   Kevin Bagatta, the president and CEO of Real Alternatives, calculates the "abortion choice percentage," which shows how many abortions are performed per 100 pregnancies. The "abortion choice percentage" is calculated by the following formula: Total Abortions / (Total Abortions + Live Births). Pennsylvania's "abortion choice percentage" was at 19.6 in 1996 when Project WIN began, and had declined to 18.9 by the year 2000. To contact Real Alternatives, go to http://www.realalternatives.org.

7   The TANF program was created by the Welfare Reform Law of 1996. It became effective July 1, 1997, and replaced what was then commonly known as welfare: Aid to Families with Dependent Children (AFDC) and the Job Opportunities and Basic Skills Training (JOBS) programs. TANF provides assistance and work opportunities to needy families by granting states the federal funds and wide flexibility to develop and implement their own welfare programs. *See* http://www.acf.hhs.gov/programs/ofa.

8   LA H.B. 1 of 2002 was signed into law on July 1, 2002.

9   An executive order issued by President George W. Bush on December 12, 2002, clarified that faith-based organizations should not be discriminated against in the implementation of social service programs "so that they may better meet social needs in America's communities." "Executive Order: Equal Protection of the Laws for Faith-Based and Community Organizations," December 12, 2002.

10 See V. Rue and A. Speckhard, "Informed Consent and Abortion: Issues in Medicine and Counseling," *Medicine & Mind* 6 (1992): 75–95.

11 *Planned Parenthood v. Casey,* 505 U.S. at 882.

12 *Barnes v. Moore,* 970 F. 2d 12 (5th Cir.), *certiorari denied,* 506 U.S. 1013 (1992).

[13] *Planned Parenthood v. Casey,* 505 U.S. at 882.

[14] *City of Akron v. Akron Center for Reproductive Health,* 462 U.S. 416 (1983). The Court has also upheld a 48-hour waiting period for minors in the context of a parental notice law. *Hodgson v. Minnesota,* 110 S.Ct. 2926 (1990).

[15] *Planned Parenthood v. Casey,* 505 U.S. at 885.

[16] The states with Women's Right to Know laws in effect or pending court challenges (indicated by*) are: AL,* AR, DE,* FL,* ID, IN, KS, KY, LA, ME, MI, MN, MS, NE, ND, OH, PA, SC, SD, UT, VA, WV, WI. For more information on state statutes or for model Women's Right to Know legislation contact legislation@unitedforlife.org or see http://www.unitedforlife.org/guides/wrtk/wrtk_main.htm.

[17] *Planned Parenthood v. Casey,* 505 U.S. at 883.

[18] Pope John Paul II, *Evangelium Vitae.*

[19] "In transforming the culture so that it supports life, women occupy a place, in thought and action, which is unique and decisive. It depends on them to promote a 'new feminism' which rejects the temptation of imitating models of 'male domination', in order to acknowledge and affirm the true genius of women in every aspect of the life of society, and overcome all discrimination, violence and exploitation." Ibid.

[20] The author wishes to thank Nikolas T. Nikas for his significant contributions to the shaping of this chapter.

Index